Power and politics in the
school system: a guidebook

KU-475-144

60 0101267 8

TELEPEN

WITHDRAWN

Power and politics in the school system: a guidebook

Michael Locke

WITHDRAWN
UNIVERSITY LIBRARY NOTTINGHAM

Routledge & Kegan Paul

London and Boston

First published in 1974
by Routledge & Kegan Paul Ltd
Broadway House, 68–74 Carter Lane
London EC4V 5EL and
9 Park Street
Boston, Mass. 02108, U.S.A.

Printed in Great Britain
by Ebenezer Baylis & Son Ltd
The Trinity Press, Worcester, and London
© Michael Locke 1974

No part of this book may be reproduced in
any form without permission from the
publisher, except for the quotation of brief
passages in criticism

ISBN 0 7100 7732 7 (C)
ISBN 0 7100 7733 5 (P)

Library of Congress Catalog Card Number: 73–89198

Contents

Contents

Part two: Education for social change

Part three: Power and participation

Introduction

Politics should be kept out of education. Education should be kept out of politics. Whichever way the statement is put, it represents a widely accepted view in education and in politics. The theme of this book is that this is neither accurate nor possible.

This book is primarily a guidebook to the school system for those who are interested or involved in it as parents, teachers, administrators, students or members of the public. It is particularly for those who want to do something – to propose reforms, to make complaints or simply to join in the arguments – and its own assumptions are that reforms are necessary in the education service. Thus its descriptions of the operation and politics of the school system become an attempt to understand not only how the system works but what effects its methods of operation have. The education service tries to avoid politics and explicit statements of objectives, and prefers to work through administrative measures. These processes tend to shut out the public and to make it difficult to argue with decisions on grounds of principle, and partly because of this they tend to be conservative. The accumulation of frustration that has been produced has led to the protests and demonstrations which have become common but which perplex educationists.

In writing a guidebook I have drawn from many sources, stealing and borrowing others' research, information and ideas. I have to offer a widespread thank-you and also to apologize to anyone who feels he has been treated unjustly. I would like to thank particularly Mary Locke, Alan Munton and Bobby Vincent-Emery for comments and criticisms on drafts, Anna Ronca for typing and Tyrrell Burgess and John Pratt of the Centre for Institutional Studies, North East London Polytechnic, where I began this book, and in thanking them I have to make it clear that none of them bear responsibility for my opinions.

Part one

The system and the consensus

1 Party politics and the Government

1 Keeping politics out of education

Everybody has opinions about education – pet theories, hunches, reasoned arguments, prejudices – and some people want their opinions to influence what happens in educational institutions. In discussing the politics of education we are therefore considering two things. First, those opinions about education and the decisions made as a consequence of them are opinions and decisions about the nature of society, now or in the future. Education both reflects current society and is a means of reforming for the future. Second, those who seek to exert influence, individually or in organizations, are involved in politics. Associations of parents, teachers, students, administrators and laymen form and seek to promote their ideas through political processes.

Given the enormous scope of these statements, the most remarkable thing about the school system is the extent to which it claims to keep politics out of education. Certain factors in the operation of the system suggest there is some truth in its claim. It is difficult to define party political differences in educational thinking, although this may be more a comment on the state of the major political parties in England and Wales. Those who work in education make a determined effort not to be pressured by opinions of the political parties, in or out of power. They attempt to make progress in education by finding a consensus of opinions, with the minimum of overt controversy, and assume that there is a mainstream of development to be followed.

During the 1960s the idea of the consensus grew and the word 'consensus' became increasingly fashionable. The concept of the consensus in education was justified both in national politics and in the unity of the education service. The greatest moments of the consensus were in the like-mindedness of the two most able ministers of education, Edward Boyle, Conservative minister from July 1962 until October 1964, and Anthony Crosland, Labour minister from

January 1965 until August 1967. Sir Edward Boyle appeared during his period of office to have accepted comprehensive schools with no less willingness than some sections of the Labour Party. Under both Boyle and Crosland the movement to comprehensive reorganization seemed not only inevitable but reasonably fast. Both ministers managed to maintain a position on education which fended off party political extremes and worked from what seemed purely educational principles. Sir Edward Boyle wrote in his foreword to the Newsom Report that 'all children should have an equal opportunity of acquiring intelligence' and was, in fact, using a phrase of Anthony Crosland's – the consensus, it was said, could not get more consensual than that.

The term 'consensus', however, does not just refer to an agreement between two ministers of education. It is difficult in the education service to act in any way which has repercussions on others without extensive consultations. The education system, as we shall see, is based on checks and balances of power and on processes of consultation and negotiation. Central government, local government, teacher unions, pressure groups and expert bodies come together to work out what is most generally agreeable. Their consultations do not operate on the simple basis of hammering out differences of opinion: there is a much more complex business of sounding out ideas, flying kites, presenting relevant facts, informal telephone conversations and avoiding confrontations. The whole is conducted with an assumption of goodwill and a common interest in the education service. Politics is interpreted as an unnecessary and unproductive rough-and-tumble.

Accompanying these processes, there has been a remarkable unanimity as to what was required in education. There has been a sense that everyone was moving in the same direction, although some would agree to differ about the pace. Expert professional opinion, regarded as politically neutral, has indicated directions for advance and these have been discussed and general agreement found before action was taken. The direction of progress is roughly leftwards politically, envisaging greater opportunity for the majority of the population, more education for everybody (without lowering the standards of the best) in order to produce a society in which everybody would be able to develop his or her natural abilities to the full and have every chance to make use of educational services regardless of his or her social circumstances. It is possible within this broad direction to emphasize the greater social justice or the economic efficiency of society. The means towards this are also subject of general agreement: raising of the school leaving age, provision of increased pre-school education (with the generally acceptable aim of reducing social disadvantage), more higher education in universities and polytechnics, smaller classes in schools, more books and equipment (particularly those using up-to-date techniques), a balance in the curriculum shifting slightly towards social relevance without losing academic standards, a more highly paid and more professional teaching force, and so on. Ministers of both major political parties would find within such objectives common ground with educational experts, administrators and teachers, the disagreements concentrating on the availability of resources to achieve them. At local government level Conservative-controlled authorities have introduced comprehensive schemes, had good relations with teachers and parents, spent money on equipment and buildings as much as Labour-controlled. Management – local authority associations – and unions have their regular confrontations in salary negotiations in the Burnham Committees but find agreement on the organization and development of education.

The achievement of the consensus is worked at; agreement is not accidental but consciously sought and efforts made to avoid political controversy in the interests of education. Warnings against political involvement made by two of the most prominent central figures in education provide examples of this. Sir William Alexander, secretary of the Association of Education Committees, wrote in *Education* (18 April 1969):

> I have the impression of an increasing party political polarization which I cannot believe is for the benefit of the education service. There can be no reasonable doubt that the organization of education cannot be changed every five years because there is a change of the political party in power. In the nature of the service there must be continuity, and to achieve effective organizational change takes a generation.... The urgent need is to get agreement on the relevant principles. This will not be helped by over-emphasis on the extreme views, either of right or left.

Lady Plowden, former chairman of the Central Advisory Council which produced the Plowden Report on primary and pre-school education, wrote in *The Times Educational Supplement* (25 August 1972):

> There is a danger that the division between the Black Paper lobby and the progressives (I hate that word) will become political, with Conservatives with a big C on one side, and Left-wingers with a big L on the other. This would be disastrous. Primary education must not become a political football.

But, as these two warnings indicate, the consensus has been dramatically challenged. In the last years of the Labour Government a group of angry conservative academics published the Black Papers in which they attacked an alleged lowering of standards, loss of traditional values, comprehensive schools and other egalitarian notions. When the first Black Paper was published in 1969, the Secretary of State for Education and Science, Edward Short, responded vigorously, attracting much attention to it and calling its publication 'one of the blackest days for education in the last one hundred years'. There was, Mr Short told the National Union of Teachers annual conference, 'a massive lurch in society towards reaction – the reaction of racism, of demands for capital and corporal punishment, of the ending of the Welfare State' and although the Black Paper was 'archaic rubbish' it should not be underestimated. The arguments from the right continued, and in 1972 its leading figures formed the National Council for Educational Standards. In 1972 a follow-up to the Black Papers was published, *Education: Threatened Standards*,[1] edited by Dr Rhodes Boyson, Chairman of the National Council for Educational Standards and a Conservative parliamentary candidate. In this one of the editors of the Black Papers, Mr A. E. Dyson, accused Edward Short and the Labour Party of standing for the destruction of almost every institution which many teachers valued and of threatening traditional standards. The Conservative Secretary of State, Mrs Margaret Thatcher, was, however, 'one of the best political guardians education has had since the war'. Mr Dyson conceived of a 'most basic and drastic choice of priorities' between educating real artists, real surgeons, real teachers and so forth or the 'anarchic utopians' encouraged by Mr Short.

The election of the Conservative Government in 1970 and the actions of its Secretary of State for Education and Science, Mrs Margaret Thatcher, encouraged the right wing. One of her first actions on taking office was to throw a spanner in the progress towards comprehensive reorganization and by upholding objections to comprehensive schemes she gave strength to local groups campaigning to save grammar schools. The combination of Black Papers, the National Council for Educational Standards and some actions of Mrs Thatcher lent respectability to reactionary thinking in education. The educational establishment, somewhat surprised, adjusted slightly to maintain a central position but did not respond dramatically. However, it is itself challenged by a growth of new political movements in education. The education service, as other public services, has been challenged by the growth of pressure groups and by increasingly vocal and articulate demands for greater participation in decision-making. Parents have organized into local and national groups, pressing for certain educational reforms as well as for their involvement in education. From the various bases of community politics, democratic control and the consumer movement there have come demands that the education service should be open to and influenced by outside groups. These have directly and implicitly challenged the consensus politics and the sense of unity within the service. Thus in discussing the politics of education one has to talk more and more about the distribution of power in the education system.

2 Party politics

The consensus has been challenged but it is still difficult to define the issues between the major political parties. Comprehensive reorganization, probably the most emotionally and politically loaded educational issue of our times, is not fought on straight party political principles, despite Mrs Thatcher's polarization of the protagonists. The Labour Party is now entirely committed to comprehensive schools but so are many elements within the Conservative Party, and deputations have come from Conservative-controlled councils to protest at the Conservative Secretary of State's failure to approve all of their comprehensive schemes. Mrs Thatcher's discouragement of comprehensive schools and her objections to a national comprehensive system sharpened local battles, but her junior minister,

Lord Belstead, gave assurances that the Conservative Government was not opposed to comprehensive schools as such. Other parliamentary battles seldom touch issues of principle and are more typically like those allegations of Conservative interference in schools by organizing political conferences in schools or about the supply of free milk in primary schools, the 'Mrs Thatcher, milk-snatcher' row.

It is possible to identify differences in philosophy between the Conservative and Labour Parties, rather than differences in educational policy. They are only really, however, the kind of differences one assumes between more left-wing and more right-wing ideas, and are not strong enough to override the business of government by consensus. One may assume Conservative preferences for the academic tradition, for freedom of choice, for paying particular attention to the education of an élite, for education as a process of selecting leaders and experts, for conceiving of a limited pool of ability among people, for meritocracy or even aristocracy. One may assume Labour preferences for egalitarianism, for a concern for the majority of people, for the underprivileged or for the bright working-class child, for socialism, for humane rather than selfish virtues. Under the Labour Government of 1964–70 expenditure on education overtook that on defence. Both parties use the arguments of industrial and economic progress and of human development in support of demands for more education. Perhaps the Conservative Party tends rather to react to proposals than to offer fresh solutions, but the Labour Party, as Rodney Barker shows in his study,[2] has been mostly concerned to extend the opportunities of the existing system to more people than to offer radical ideas of what education could be.

Occasionally there are demonstrations of such differences in philosophy. In October 1969 Mr Edward Short, Labour Secretary of State, referred to traditional exams as 'a millstone round the necks of the schools' and hoped that before long people in education would apply themselves 'to ridding our secondary schools of the tyranny of the examination'. Mrs Margaret Thatcher, on the other hand, had doubts about 'new-fangled' methods. In practice, however, neither's period of office provided strong examples of distinctively Labour or Conservative policies, and even a leading member of the Labour Party was reduced to defining the differences between the parties in terms of personality: 'the difference between Mrs Thatcher and Ted Short'.

The party manifestos have not provided in specific proposals any very different commitments between the Labour and Conservative Parties. In 1970 the main issues were common – more resources for nursery and primary education, raising of the leaving age to sixteen, expansion for further and higher education. Labour pledged a new Education Act which would include a requirement that local authorities introduce comprehensive schemes and which would also bring parents into the partnership of running schools. Conservatives pledged freedom for local authorities to decide on their own secondary school system and freedom of choice for parents. The Liberal Party supported comprehensives, more resources for primary and nursery and more opportunity for further education outside university.

As the secretary of the Association of Education Committees, Sir William Alexander, commented at the time (*Education*, 29 May 1970):

> It is true that there are differences of emphasis in the two major political parties, but it is also true that both are completely committed to the development of the education service, and indeed both recognize the vital contribution which the service must make to secure the economic prosperity and the social stability of the nation. The fundamental problem, as always, is how to secure sufficient financial support to enable the policies on which the nation is agreed to be carried into effect.

He concluded:

> In short, the need is not for a competition between the political parties. So far as education is concerned, the need is rather for maximum co-operation to try to secure a plan which will enable the agreed policies to be carried into effect with the support of all political parties and with the necessary resources of money and manpower.

Two issues are exceptions to this likemindedness and have aroused more passions. Through the 1950s and 1960s the Labour Party became concerned, in some cases obsessed, about independent and public schools. These appeared as the bulwark of privilege and class differentiation in society defended by the Conservative Party: at a time when many social inequalities were diminished, it was still possible for the rich to buy a possibly superior and certainly prestigious education for their children; at a time when state education could provide the best, it was still possible to buy social and academic status. Demands from the rank and file of the Labour Party that independent schools should be closed down were never taken as practical politics, however, and there were differences of opinions between those who would abolish them, those who would integrate them and those who would simply take away any tax advantages and ignore them. Mr Anthony Crosland, when Labour's Secretary of State for Education, established the Public Schools Commission to propose ways in which the public schools could be rendered harmless. Its proposals in its first report (the Newsom Report, 1968, to be distinguished from the Newsom Report, 1963, on thirteen- to sixteen-year-olds of average or less than average ability) and in its second report on direct grant and independent day schools (the Donnison Report) were intended to be practical but were never near being implemented. The Newsom Report proposed that a number of public schools should be integrated and make half their places available to state pupils. The objection to independent and public schools remained strong in the Labour Party but the hoped-for final solution became to sqeeze them and progressively fade out or integrate them. The idea was to combine an end to their charitable status with tougher criteria for recognition.

A second issue was that of the Open University, a remarkable and uncharacteristic story in terms of its political conception and administrative and political survival. Proposed as the University of the Air in a speech by Mr Harold Wilson, it became the Open University and was actually established, somewhat against the odds, at a time of economic stringency and cuts in other areas of education. It survived the January 1968 cuts, which delayed the raising of the school leaving age and restricted resources on further and adult education. It had acquired vibrations of the soul of the Labour Party by offering university education, traditionally the preserve of the privileged, to those people who had missed out earlier in life; it was the 'university of the second chance'. It acquired, furthermore, the ardent support of Miss Jennie Lee as junior minister in the Department of Education and Science and maverick support from influential civil servants within the department. It was also close to Prime Minister Harold Wilson's heart. When the Conservative Government took office in 1970 there were doubts about its future, but it survived. The Open University won acceptance by not being as radical a departure in higher education as some of its early ideals suggested: it has extended opportunity but its attitude to education is academic and it is, like all universities, concerned above all with standards; it has not taken dramatic numbers of working-class students.

The most overtly party political acts of the post-1970 Conservative Secretary of State for Education, Mrs Margaret Thatcher, were her actions against comprehensive reorganization. Shortly after taking office she cancelled Circular 10/65 in which the Labour Government had requested local education authorities to present schemes for going comprehensive, by issuing Circular 10/70. This much had been anticipated but in two other actions, administratively based actions, Mrs Thatcher took further her discouragement of comprehensive schools. First, in keeping with the manifesto she concentrated building resources on primary schools to replace schools built before 1903, with the effect of stopping resources for secondary school building except in areas of rising population and this hindered some authorities' plans to build comprehensive schools. Second, through her interpretation of Section 13 of the Education Act 1944 she encouraged local groups to object to comprehensive schemes on behalf of particular grammar schools.

The Conservative Government also introduced a major White Paper in December 1972, *Education: A Framework for Expansion*,[3] discussed in the next section of this chapter, which proposed expansion of nursery education, reorganization of the colleges of education and expansion of higher education in polytechnics more than in universities.

The major responses of the Labour Party in Opposition were – when its leadership thought about anything else than how difficult it was to have been the Government and how unjust it was to be no longer – directed predictably at the principles involved in Mrs Thatcher's actions on comprehensive reorganization and at the use of resources in the White Paper. Labour argued that it made insufficient resources available and was too long in its implementation. Its spokesman on education for the first years of the Government, Mr Edward Short, also offered the general criticisms that the Government was ignoring the evidence on social deprivation and educational disadvantage and failing to give sufficient extra resources to priority areas. The main attacks on Mrs Thatcher came, in fact, not from the Labour Party but from educational organizations and their leaders who explicitly and implicitly accused her of being reactionary and hindering the progressive development of the education service.

There were at the time, however, new education policies being developed by working parties within the Labour Party. In a document, *Labour's Programme for Britain*, put to its annual conference in 1972, were proposals not only to establish a comprehensive system but to discourage streaming in schools and to abolish GCE examinations. ('Examinations exert a disproportionate influence in the curriculum; tend to be inflexible and irrelevant; and reinforce social divisions.') Independent schools would have to be licensed pending their eventual abolition. The programme proposed educational provision to be extended for the under-fives, at higher education level and for adults and set out a comprehensive system of schools and further education colleges for the sixteen to eighteen age-group. Its general sentiments were fairly radical:

> We hope that, when Labour returns to power, resolute Government and local authority action in these directions (comprehensive reorganization and in deprived areas positive discrimination), will be matched by an equal determination on the part of schools and colleges themselves, to humanize authoritarian regimes where they still exist, to reconsider such educationally deleterious practices as streaming by ability, and to give pupils and students both practice in democratic decision making and teaching about the machinery of democracy.

The proposals illustrate the idea of progressiveness in education. The degree to which they became controversial would depend largely on the speed and rigour of their implementation. In government the party would, as the statement above recognizes, be constrained by the independence of local authorities and schools. The proposals for a sixteen to eighteen comprehensive system represented a logical evolution in bringing school and further education together (see chapter 8). They would be radical if they developed the further education tradition over that of the grammar school sixth form and more controversial if they were pushed through before local authorities, unions, headteachers and principals had had the time to be persuaded of the justice or inevitability of the plans. It is interesting that one of its proposals, that for continued education to the age of eighteen, was included in the Education Act 1918 and the Education Act 1944 but had not to date been put into practice.

The thinking of these proposals was developed further by a Labour Party Green Paper[4] produced by a study group chaired by Geoffrey Rhodes, MP. It envisaged post-school education in two comprehensive sectors, a tertiary sector for sixteen to eighteen and an adult education sector for all over eighteen including universities, further and adult education. It implied, whilst hedging from a directly controversial statement, that the universities would lose their favoured position on resources and prestige – although Labour's shadow minister of education at the time, Roy Hattersley, argued that far from giving the universities less, further and adult education would be given more, that there would be more resources for education. The Labour Green Paper stated as its principle: 'We envisage an open system of post-school education where opportunities are accessible to all and the resources available shared by all wishing to further their education.' These controversies of further and higher education are echoed in the debates about school education; there, too, democratic arguments have developed from the equitable sharing of resources to the concern for open and accessible provision (chapter 8).

3 Central government

It is usual to view with scepticism the manifestos of political parties, no less with educational topics than with others. The main problem of the party in government has lately appeared to be that of governing at all rather than of putting its principles into effect. But this is not simply a matter of keeping the education service ticking over. As we discussed earlier in this chapter, the education service assumes a continuous development towards more progressive ideas, and thus the problem of governing is partly to resolve conflicting opinions into the consensus. It is also to secure enough resources for the expansion of the education service, which all assume is natural and right; in times of crisis it may be to prevent cuts but more often it is to attain a rate of expansion.

The principal political battle between Government and Opposition is therefore a consistent one, the battle over whether the Government is putting enough resources into education as against the Opposition's promise of more. The national politics of education appear not so much as issues of principle, but concern about the relations between Secretary of State and his Department on one hand and the Treasury, Cabinet and other spending departments on the other.

The Secretary of State for Education and Science becomes in this battle for resources not so much a temporary and politically committed boss, but a representative and leader of the education service as a whole, almost a constitutional monarch. Within the education service there is a sense of everybody pulling together in the same boat and they all expect the Secretary of State to do his bit at the prow, as battering-ram or figurehead. Perhaps some of the annoyance with Mrs Thatcher is explained in these terms: when she was appointed it became evident that she did not share the vaguely progressive assumptions of the service, but when she published her White Paper it became clear that she (or her officials) had managed to get secure resources for education and then much of the hostility evaporated.

The Secretary of State for Education who came off worst of all in the eyes of the education service was Labour's Mr Patrick Gordon Walker. He was believed to have betrayed the education service by acceding in January 1968 to the postponement of raising the school leaving age. It was commonly agreed in education that his commitment should have been to the service rather than national economic policy.

A further factor in central government is the DES. It is considered to have responsibility not simply for pen-pushing administration but for the development of the education service, for encouraging good practice within it and, of course, with the Secretary of State, for securing resources. The impact of the DES on what happens in schools is hard to define. It certainly is not a direct relationship, although its administrative guidance and controls have both an educational basis and educational effects. They are limited in number, but in school building, for example, the cost limits, standards and advice provided by the DES is crucial for what can be done in schools, hence for their teaching methods and curricula. The schools are administered by local education authorities and responsibility for curricula and teaching methods lies in the schools, but the responsibility which the DES assumes for their development is evident behind the scenes. (It is as faulty to blame or credit the DES with whatever is done in schools as it is to accept at face value its absence of formal responsibilities.) The DES would maintain that it was neutral except in being concerned for the development of education. What it does consider its role is to bring people together, to sift opinions, to achieve the consensus and to disseminate its findings in the hope of persuading people.

In December 1972 the DES published a White Paper on the development of aspects of the education service into the 1980s, and it was a document of the DES rather than of the Conservative Secretary of State. Its origins went back to the late 1960s and the intention of the Labour Government to produce a Green Paper on higher education and a new Education Act to replace the Education Act 1944. The logistics of preparing the White Paper were of as many as two or three score civil servants devoting substantial parts of their time for over two years. They collected evidence and opinions from educational organizations, unions, pressure groups and experts. They distilled them and assessed their implications for expenditure. They drafted recommendations and related sectional proposals to an overall policy. They negotiated resources with the Treasury. The White Paper's proposals are not specifically Conservative but represent the achievement of a consensus and the securing of resources to gain its objectives.

There were two major sections in the White Paper, the reorganization of the colleges of education and the expansion of preschool education. The first was the product of a dissatisfaction with the existing arrangements for teacher training which had received public attention in the late 1960s. In 1969 a Select Committee of the House of Commons, chaired by Fred Willey, MP, had begun an investigation of teacher training, and a rival inquiry was conducted within the area training organizations at the instigation of the Secretary of State, Mr Edward Short. A pressure group called SPERTTT (Society for the Promotion of Educational Reform Through Teacher Training) provided a focus for demands for radical changes, and the Association of Teachers in Colleges and Departments of Education presented its expert opinion and defended its members' interests. All this encouraged a public debate, in newspapers, specialist journals, public meetings and books, but before the issues were resolved, the Conservative Government had taken office and appointed an official inquiry under the chairmanship of Lord James. This inquiry therefore already had a great deal of information and advice with which to work, and educational organizations and unions in turn presented their evidence to it. When the James Report was published there was further public discussion, and unions and other bodies commented on it to the Secretary of State. Over a year later the product of all this was issued as the recommendations of the White Paper, which was then further debated before the DES took action.

The second major set of proposals was for an expansion of pre-school, particularly nursery, education. In order to put resources into this area the expansion of higher education had had to be slowed down, and in the months leading up to the White Paper there often appeared to be a straightforward battle between the protagonists of universities – the Association of University Teachers and the Committee of Vice-Chancellors and Principals – and the National Campaign for Nursery Education. The outcome was a victory for the nursery campaign, though it was not as harsh upon the universities as they had feared. The pre-school lobby had emerged with the perfect political issue of the times, and it was hard to attack it without seeming to put the boot in on little children. The Plowden Report in 1967 and research findings had emphasized the importance of the early years of a child's development and the educational problems of cultural and social deprivation at that age, and these arguments combined with the interests of women of all classes who wanted or needed to work. It would still be, however, the early 1980s before the recommendations of the Plowden Report had been implemented – and it was by no means clear that the greatest benefit would accrue to underprivileged children.

The Labour Party's reaction was muted, concerned mostly that nursery education was not going to be established fast enough and quarrelling with the figures. Mr Short was reduced to complaining in *The Times Higher Education Supplement* (15 December 1972) that it was 'a superficially attractive document which palls with further acquaintance'.

The White Paper illustrates one aspect of the officials' dominance over politicians. In the business of running an education service, of taking opinions, of consultations and of finding areas of general agreement about progress, of securing resources, permanent officials are in a much stronger position than ministers. The opinions of what they tend to refer to as their 'political masters' are in fact only one element which officials take into account when assessing directions in which to proceed. Even in the unarguably political acts of the two circulars on comprehensive schools, Labour's 10/65 and Conservative's 10/70, the administrative style of the Department and its partnership with the local education authorities moulded what the ministers wanted to say. Just as 10/65 'requested' local authorities to prepare comprehensive plans and refrained from infringing local authority autonomy by any compulsion, so 10/70 only reiterated local authority autonomy. The principles of the Secretary are implied rather than stated directly – everybody knew what Mr Crosland and Mrs Thatcher were about – but a problem is that the minister lacks ways of officially promulgating the principles upon which he is working. The determination of Mrs Thatcher's methods of action against comprehensives only slowly became evident as people saw how she was using the procedures of approving comprehensive schemes and the appeals procedure of Section 13 of the Education Act 1944. And because it was done by administrative measures it became harder to argue about, to assert other principles. In strict administrative terms each individual school's reorganization was considered separately as was statutorily required, rather than schemes and overall plans or objectives, and by Section 13 parents' objections had to be heard. On one level the Secretary of State was only following procedures strictly; whenever protests reached a certain point she allowed the objections and preserved the grammar school – what could be political about that?

References

1 R. Boyson (ed.), *Education: Threatened Standards*, Churchill Press, Enfield, 1972.
2 R. Barker, *Education and Politics 1900–1951*, Oxford University Press, London, 1972.
3 *Education: A Framework for Expansion* (White Paper), HMSO, London, 1972.
4 *Higher and Further Education – Report of a Labour Party Study Group* (Opposition Green Paper), Labour Party, London, 1973.

2 The system and local government

1 Local authorities and partnership

Central government does not run the schools. It is local education authorities that build most of the schools, finance them, appoint and pay the teachers, supply the books and equipment, are responsible for the upkeep of the buildings and enforce attendance at them by children of school age. It is LEAS which determine the character of their schools and provide a local education service in schools, colleges and other institutes.

The education system is usually described as a 'partnership' of central government and LEAS. Responsibility and power are shared, and one of the effects of this is that it is difficult to pinpoint where in the system specific decisions are made. This makes it a perplexing organization to deal with, and often a frustrating one if action is being sought. The tendency for political pressure to be directed at the Secretary of State in person adds to this because in most cases he can quite simply brush off complaints, attacks and proposals as not being his responsibility. Likewise an LEA may claim it is prevented from acting by restrictions and pressures of central government. These confusions are, however, on the whole a product of the virtues of the system.

The education system is usually described as 'a national service locally administered'. The Secretary of State for Education and Science is given this overall duty by the Education Act 1944: 'To secure the effective execution by local education authorities, under his control and direction, of a national policy for providing a varied and comprehensive educational service in every area.' At first sight these seem like overbearing powers but in fact the Secretary of State only has real statutory power in a few specific ways stated in the Act. These concern the setting of standards, arbitration in disputes, decisions on opening, closing and changing the nature of schools and the possibility of intervening if the local authority acts unreasonably. The overall statement, none the less, does tend to set the tone of the partnership between DES and LEAS, and central government has acquired a slightly more dominant position over the years. The autonomy of local authorities is, however, stubbornly protected, and whether they accept the Department's guidance or pressure is ultimately their choice.

LEAS are, after the reorganization of local government in April 1974, the 104 counties, metropolitan districts, London boroughs and Inner London Education Authority. Each of these has an education committee, as required by the Local Government Act 1972, and has appointed a chief education officer or director of education and a staff of assistant education officers, inspectors, organizers and advisers, school meals organizers, administrative assistants and other ancillary officers. LEAS maintain schools out of the income from rates and from central government's rate support grant. LEAS have all the statutory powers and duties to provide school education.

In being run by local authorities the local education service is governed by local government as well as education legislation. Local authorities can only act in ways allowed for in acts of parliament – just as the powers and duties to run an education service depend upon the Education Act of 1944. This constraint upon their actions is usually seen in terms of its financial implications: local authorities can only spend money in ways which are allowed by act of parliament. An official appointed by the Department of the Environment, the district auditor, checks local authority accounts. If he finds money has been spent *ultra vires* – outside the local authority's powers – he can make the individuals responsible pay it back. This protects against fraud and corruption but equally against money being spent improperly even if with good intentions. Thus there is always at the back of the minds of local authority elected members and officials the fear that if they exceed the powers given them in acts of parliament they may have to pay up out of their own pockets. This gives central government through parliament an ultimate power over local authorities, examples of which were seen in its legislation against the provision of free school milk and on council house rents in the Housing Finance Act.

The controls which the DES and central government have over the administration of schools and colleges are limited, mostly financial and negative. For new school buildings LEAS need the permission of the Department of the Environment to borrow the capital required to finance them and have to gain the approval of the DES for the plans. The DES sets cost limits and minimum standards, specifying such things as playground and teaching space and other facilities. On teacher employment the DES takes part in the pay negotiations in the Burnham Committee – indicating the global sum which the LEAS as employers can offer – and sets a quota of teachers for each authority. (The total supply of teachers is controlled by the DES through the colleges of education.) The other major controls are those of central government over total local authority spending and, to a certain extent, over the broad ways in which it is spent. The Government makes a rate support grant to local authorities in order to supplement the rates and to even out inequalities between rich and poor areas. This grant now accounts for about 60 per cent of local authority expenditure. It is negotiated between the local authority national associations and the Department of the Environment with the involvement of the DES. This tends to fix total local authority spending – though they can spend more by increasing the rates – and gives central government some influence on how the money is being spent although theoretically it is given without strings.

The DES issues guidance to local authorities over a much wider range of topics as part of its responsibility for a national pattern of education. It does this formally through circulars and administrative memoranda. The latter are usually concerned with detailed topics or minor revisions of current practice. Circulars are more significant, possibly asking for information, suggesting action or proposing how legislation should be implemented. LEAS can ignore circulars, as some did Circular 10/65 on comprehensive reorganization, but on the whole they go along with them. Circulars are, in fact, usually the product of consultations between the DES and interested parties, including the local authority associations, and so it is assumed that circulars are widely acceptable before they are issued. There are also less formal means of communication between DES and LEAS, means of offering guidance or putting on pressure. Officers of DES and LEAS are in touch with each other; HM inspectors (HMIS) carry advice from the centre out to LEAS and schools; ministers make public speeches indicating new directions which an authority, with no compulsion, may accept as progress with which they should be in step. When the situation is particularly sensitive a deputation from the LEA may visit the DES.

Another important element in the partnership are the national local authority associations which, before local government re-organization in April 1974, were the Association of Municipal Corporations, the County Councils Association and the Association of Education Committees. The DES would normally consult these bodies as representing local authority opinion. In his study of Edward Boyle and Anthony Crosland as ministers of education, Maurice Kogan[1] reports that:

> Neither Crosland nor Boyle would have thought to move very far without consulting Sir William Alexander, Secretary to the Association of Education Committees, Sir Ronald Gould, Secretary to the National Union of Teachers, and their counterparts in the other local authority and teachers' organizations. Such officials as William Alexander constitute a powerful – perhaps the most powerful – entity within the education service for a far longer period than any Minister or Permanent Secretary and most senior officials within the Department. They know well the service for which they work and command trust and respect from those whom they represent.

By these means is the partnership maintained. Local authorities do not have complete freedom of action, yet they are not instructed what to do. The DES and Secretary of State is not a dictator but nor is it only a co-ordinator. Although legislation – acts of parliament and statutory instruments – is limited, there is a web of guidance and pressures. The theme is consultation. Although the central government has sanctions available, usually it is the force of argument and wish to co-operate that are effective. DES and LEAS are unwilling to disturb their working relationship.

2 Church and private

The situation is further complicated by church and private schools. During the nineteenth century the church authorities established their separate education services. The Education Act 1870 which established school boards, the first public authorities for education, did so in order to supplement church provision. The Education Acts 1902 and 1944 integrated church schools into the state system. In 1971 of over 28,000 schools in England and Wales there were just under 9,000 belonging to church authorities. Church schools retain their identity in one of three ways. 'Voluntary controlled' schools are little different in practice from ordinary local authority – 'county' – schools except that a third of the governors or managers may be from the church – 'voluntary' – body. The governors (secondary schools) or managers (primary) must be consulted over the appointment of headteachers and teachers giving denominational instruction. 'Voluntary aided' schools have two-thirds of the governors or managers from the voluntary body. Governors or managers control religious instruction and in secondary schools the whole curriculum and are responsible for maintenance and new building (though assisted by a grant). There are also a few 'special agreement' schools set up under the Education Act 1936.

Most voluntary controlled schools are Church of England, as are half of the voluntary aided. Roman Catholic schools are all aided or special agreement except one. There are also a few Jewish and other denomination schools. About nine out of ten voluntary schools are primary.

The voluntary bodies responsible for these schools add still further to the amount of consultation in the education system. For example, the reorganization of the colleges of education proposed by the White Paper 1972 required negotiations and agreement with Church of England and Roman Catholic bodies. In some authorities voluntary schools have created problems in going comprehensive when governing bodies have wished to preserve the status of their grammar schools, and the LEA cannot compel them to join the scheme.

A few endowed grammar schools also have voluntary aided status, the voluntary body being a foundation of perhaps a city company, and some of these have decided that to go comprehensive would offend all their principles.

Private schools are independent of the DES and LEAs although they need to be registered with the DES and may be 'recognized as efficient'. A number of associations represent their interests including the Headmasters' Conference (HMC) that of the public schools, the Independent Association of Preparatory Schools (IAPS) that of the prep schools. Direct grant schools are 179 (in 1971) independent schools involved in the state system. They are mostly grammar schools and are fee-paying schools which make available a proportion of their places to the local authority in return for a grant direct from the DES. They are a rather more controversial feature particularly in comprehensive reorganization; they continue to be selective schools, thus tending to cream off some of the brightest pupils from comprehensives. The Inner London Education Authority therefore decided to take up no more places at direct grant schools. Direct grant schools defend themselves as offering freedom of choice to parents and academic standards, as the letter from the High Master of Manchester Grammar School quoted in chapter 6 (p. 91) shows.

3 Ideas and inhibitions

We have seen how the education system comprises a partnership of DES and LEAs, a relationship in which suggestions and pressures may be as significant as clear-cut decisions and regulations. There is a mutual interest in maintaining the relationship, and this is in some cases made even more complicated by allegiances to church or independent school ethos. On its creditable side the system entails a high degree of consultation, a movement with the consensus; it is perpetually middle-of-the-road.

These things concern the administration of schools, the facilities with which they work and the framework in which they operate. Teaching methods and curriculum are, however, largely the responsibility of the individual schools. It is the LEA's responsibility to keep them up to standard and they are inspected by HMIs who are attached to the DES. The only curriculum prescribed by law is the inclusion of religious education in the Education Act 1944. The subjects taught in schools and the curriculum are the responsibility of the school and of its managers or governors; in effect, usually the responsibility of its headteacher. Syllabuses are determined by university-based boards or, in the case of the Certificate of Secondary Education by boards working under the aegis of the Schools Council.

Some of the reasons for this are discussed in chapter 5, above all that teachers as professionals are considered to be the proper and most likely people to develop ideas and to know how to teach. Ideas and innovations are expected to come from the schools and work upwards to local education office and to DES rather than vice versa, and the teacher unions are able to play a role in this as discussed in chapter 3. To assist in the development of new methods and new ideas the Schools Council was established, and through various research projects on curriculum matters it suggests improved or more up-to-date ways of teaching. Within university departments of education and colleges of education research projects, financed by foundations, perform a similar function.

Early in 1973 there were protests from the Labour Party that certain schools had taken part in politically biased conferences organized by the Conservative Party. The Secretary of State for Education turned aside criticisms by explaining schools' independence on curriculum (letter to Roy Hattersley, MP, 17 January 1973: Press release):

> From time to time I receive from Members of Parliament allegations of political bias either in teaching or in the materials and methods used for teaching. In every case I have to reply in the same way pointing out that Parliament has not given a Secretary of State any relevant powers of direction over the secular instruction given in maintained schools. . . .
> The general form of the rules (of management) and articles (of government) was settled by negotiation between the Government, the local authority associations and representatives of the churches. Broadly speaking their effect is that the curriculum is subject to the control of the local education authority in a primary school and of the governors in a secondary school.

> From the debates on Section 23 when the Bill (the Education Act 1944) was passing through the House it seems to have been the intention that the governors would have the general direction of the curriculum as actually given from day to day within the school; and the headteacher would have the responsibility to carry out the curriculum in the sense desired by the governing body.

> There are no statutory provisions regarding political bias. By custom it is well understood that teachers whatever their

personal political sympathies or activities have a duty in their professional capacity to be impartial. In discharging this duty it is expected that taking the syllabus as a whole they will maintain a proper balance in their choice and use of materials and resources. The judgment on this matter is entrusted to the teachers themselves in the first instance.

In the light of the matter set out above, I have considered the Stevenage conference which you referred to me. This should be tested and judged in the same way as other available teaching resources. It is for the teachers who attended the conference with their pupils to consider whether it was biased and if so to take appropriate steps to restore the balance.

Similar arguments apply to new methods as much as to political bias. The process of introducing new ideas into schools is a slow and somewhat random affair. There is no instruction from central government, though the DES officials may commend certain ideas and encourage them through personal contacts and through the inspectorate. LEA inspectors, advisers and organizers will also transmit new ideas. Teacher centres and in-service training for teachers will help ideas to spread. The need to have some pupils pass exams is a constraint on teachers, as are inspections by HMIs. Thus much depends upon informal processes – upon personal meetings, private discussions, for example – rather than upon public statements and formal communications. If we put this together with the partnership of DES and LEAs, we build up a picture of a total service in which little is clear-cut. In the operation of the system teachers, administrators and politicians all prefer informal over formal ways of doing things, hints and persuasion rather than regulations, discreet discussions rather than public confrontations. The system, as we have seen, encourages this.

The operation of the system is based on the assumption that such methods keep it flexible and responsive. A trusted individual, such as an HMI, is reckoned to be more flexible in transmitting ideas than a public statement with the commitment which that implies. He can adjust his position, keep open contacts and pass on subtleties through his expertise. Similarly in planning new developments the actual announcement, except in occasional circumstances, has often been pre-empted by the amount of administrative actions which are already moving in that direction as well as by the number of kites flown by the political leaders. All this contributes to the process of consultation.

The education service has, as we shall discuss in chapter 5, a strong sense of identity. LEAS and DES have a special relationship which transcends the divisions between other central and local departments. Education committees are not only one of the most powerful in a local council but have links with other education committees and with their chief education officers. (This may be affected by the new management techniques introduced with re-organization of local government in so far as policy committees may determine decisions on education as part of overall local authority planning. The education service, however, has resisted such developments and succeeded in keeping statutory education committees written in the Local Government Act 1972.)

The whole system therefore is not only complex and intricate but very perplexing to the outsider. The emphasis placed upon informal contacts can seem an under-the-counter deal to the outsider who is trying to identify where and how decisions are made and trying perhaps to influence them. Power is diffused between DES, LEAS and schools but also the processes of communications and advice are split into many channels. It may be more flexible than making a public statement but it is also less accessible. It means also that most discussions about objectives and methods are conducted only in the terms chosen by people within the system. There tends to be a single framework of ideas, the assumptions of which are hard to question. It makes it hard to introduce radical ideas into the debate.

The advantages of this style of administration are that there is full consultation and that it achieves a willingness of most people to act together. Partly because of the many processes and partly because of the caution of the people involved there are not generally sudden stops and starts, dramatic new directions or devastating cancellations. One always has to test the water unless you're the last in. The consensus is found but innovation is always tentative; there is an enormous inertia.

Reference

1 M. Kogan, *The Politics of Education*, Penguin, Harmondsworth, 1971, p. 32.

3 The unions

1 Membership

The third partner in the education service is the teachers and their unions. In a complex, pluralist society we do not expect either political parties or central and local government to encompass all the opinions and presentations of facts which are needed to contribute to the development of institutions. We look to unions and pressure groups to form, to represent their members' interests and to make available the expertise of their members. The teachers' unions act on a far wider range of subjects than the sectional interests of their members on pay and employer–employee relations. They have become a vital part of the education service in their representation of professional views on education.

In a study of teachers' unions R. D. Coates[1] reported that three out of four teachers belonged to one of the major unions and that 'school teachers are amongst the most highly organized of English workers'. The unions present the opinions of classroom teachers on developments, have built up formidable and highly influential organizations, and are an essential part of the processes of consultation. In his study of Edward Boyle and Anthony Crosland as ministers of education, Maurice Kogan[2] includes teachers' union leaders with local authority representatives as people whom the minister would always consult, as quoted in the last chapter. As influential professional bodies, the teachers' unions not only put forward their views about education to central and local government, they also are committed to the education service in itself. In other employments unions may be primarily engaged in a battle on behalf of their members with the employers, but in teaching the unions and employers stress their common interest in education above any differences over pay or working conditions. Nationally and locally the unions regard it as part of their function to proselytize for education and to support or chivvy the Secretary of State with demands for more resources for education.

The dominant union is the NUT with a total membership which reached 340,000 in its centenary year, 1970. It has lost several thousand since then but with over 230,000 in service in 1972 it has the majority of all teachers in primary and in secondary schools. It has a staff of more than 160 officers and offers a range of services from legal advice and support on professional matters to educational research and publishing, including a weekly newspaper the *Teacher*. It has over 1,100 local associations formed into divisions corresponding with the new local government areas.

Its rival, though considerably smaller with 56,000 members in 1972, is the National Association of Schoolmasters. It has an office staff of three dozen. The NAS has a history of greater militancy than the NUT, having engaged frequently in strikes or working to contract, and has gained members accordingly. All its members are men and two-thirds of them are in secondary schools. It represents the interests of the 'career teacher' and thus usually differs from the NUT in the salary claim made by the unions in negotiations with the employers (the LEAs) in the Burnham Committee. Career teachers have their interests best served by salary scales with a high maximum to which they work over a number of years whereas young teachers and those only in the profession for a few years are benefited by higher salaries at the start and less differentials. The NAS in salary negotiations accuses the NUT of being dominated by primary school teachers and young women who leave the profession after a few years, and claims that in serving their interests the NUT fails to help teachers become a well-paid profession. The NAS is often identified as more reactionary than the NUT as well as more militant, although the NAS believes it is simply being more realistic and defending better the interests of the classroom teacher. It can also accuse the NUT locally and nationally of being dominated by headteachers, of whom there is a preponderance on the national executive committee, and of therefore being less likely to rock the boat. The reputation of the NAS as reactionary is founded on such things as its allegations of increased violence in schools and its scepticism on raising the school leaving age. NAS members tend to adopt a more 'no-nonsense' attitude and, confronted with the conventional wisdom on the relationship between social deprivation and educational disadvantage, are more likely to demand an assertion of moral and academic standards and a tough line with trouble-makers.

The NAS has in the past opposed equal pay for women, it having been formed by a breakaway from the NUT in 1922. It is not now opposed to equal pay as such but argues that the career teacher, who is more likely to be male, should be better rewarded. In 1967 it assisted in the formation of a sister union, the Union of Women Teachers to represent the interests of women career teachers. At the beginning of 1973 the UWT had just over 14,000 full members.

The other unions in state schools live rather more under the shadow of the NUT. A group known as the Joint Four comprises the Association of Head Mistresses, the Head Masters' Association, the Assistant Mistresses Association and the Assistant Masters' Association. Their memberships from the secondary schools, particularly the grammar schools, were reported in March 1973 as Assistant Masters' Association – nearly 38,000, Assistant Mistresses Association – about 30,000, Head Masters' Association – about 1,800, and Association of Head Mistresses – 810 members and 80 affiliates (senior mistresses in mixed schools and headmasters of girls' schools). The National Association of Head Teachers, originally a group within the NUT, has 16,500 members. A very recent breakaway from the NUT is the Professional Association of Teachers which had grown two years after its inaugural meeting in September 1970 to over 5,000 members.

In further and higher education there are different unions, the largest being the Association of Teachers in Technical Institutions, the Association of Teachers in Colleges and Department of Education, the Association of University Teachers and the National Union of Students.

2 Work

We can look at what the teachers' unions do in two parts, as suggested at the beginning of the chapter, in connection with pay and employer–employee relations and in connection with educational matters.

Teachers' salaries are negotiated in the Burnham Committee. This comprises 28 representatives of the teachers, 26 representatives of the local authorities and 2 representatives of the DES. Of the teachers 16 are from the NUT and 3 from the NAS, and the teachers are led by

Burnham Cmttee

the general secretary of the NUT. The whole committee also splits into two, the Teachers' Panel and the Management Panel, which meet separately, the first to work out the claim which the teachers should submit and the second to work out the response. The negotiations in full committee and in panels continue over several months, and when they break down the claim is put to a separate arbitration tribunal. The procedures have not worked well in recent years, there having been a series of stalemates and confrontations between teachers and management, as well as the disagreements within the teachers' ranks between NUT and NAS. On the teachers' side there has been a growth of militancy in support of their pay claims. The first NUT strikes were in 1969. In July militants persuaded London teachers to close 200 schools for a half-day. In November the union, in concert with the NAS and later the AMA, began a series of fortnight-long and lightning strikes in selections of LEAS. They escalated them until at the beginning of March 1970 the Secretary of State, Edward Short, intervened and told the management that an interim increase would be acceptable. Having won the case, the unions were given confidence for future direct actions.

One factor which affected the teachers' pay negotiations was the increasing national economic stringency in which the management were limited by the DES and Treasury and by the Government's pay and prices policies. Thus teachers' unions to press their case needed to act upon the Government as a whole. One of the ways they sought to do this was by joining the TUC and another was expressing their feelings and hoping to influence public opinion through strikes, marches and demonstrations.

The NAS has also undertaken direct action in support of its members in other matters. For example, in Teesside in December 1972 NAS and UWT members worked to contract in defence of colleagues whose status was affected by reorganization of their schools into comprehensives. The rising militancy among trade unions as a whole is also reflected in demands from the left-wing and Rank and File group within the NUT for direct action against conditions in schools. But the majority of the unions' work in the areas of employer–employee relations is through casework for individuals and through committees such as the joint working group on employer–employee relations.

The range of education issues covered by the teachers' unions is very wide, covering most or all current concerns. Policies are formally made at annual conferences but they are developed and sophisticated through working parties and committees within the unions and by their officials. The unions are consulted by or offer advice to central and local government and undertake research on an enormous variety of topics, far wider than is ever discussed at any one conference. A vital part of the processes of consultation is not just the opinions the unions have to offer but the research and technical information with which they support them. The unions present their views and their information through lobbying, publicity, membership of committees, deputations, their MPs or other contacts in parliament and by direct contact with officials. At central government level the contacts of unions with ministers and officials which make the news are official deputations, but the main purpose of these appears to be those occasions when formal statements of differences of opinion need to be made and seen by the union membership to have been made. They are formal and not necessarily very useful. The productive work, such are the friendly relations of DES and the major unions, is done on a day-to-day basis between officials over the phone or in private meetings. Ronald Manzer in his study of the NUT[3] comments that 'an educational pressure group must convince the civil servants' and that this is achieved by private consultations rather than 'ritualistic' deputations. The DES works also through temporary or permanent working parties and advisory committees, for example on educational technology and the school health service, and these include representatives of the unions. A further part of these processes of consultation and achieving consensus is that the DES sends out drafts of its proposed circulars for comment. In 1971, for example, the NUT commented on circulars about the education of autistic children, standards for school premises, work experience, raising the school leaving age and on children with learning difficulties. The last was so criticized by the unions and other bodies consulted that it was never issued, despite the fact that the Secretary of State, Mrs Thatcher, had indicated a circular would be published on the subject. The NUT's comments on the draft of Circular 10/65 persuaded Mr Anthony Crosland to include the need for LEAs to consult teachers in preparing comprehensive school schemes. The unions also react in public to any major items of Government policy, for example, welcoming and criticizing various aspects of the White Paper issued in 1972. The NUT disapproved of its figures on teacher supply and made this known by press statements, letters to the DES, a deputation to the Secretary of State, a research report on the subject and pressure in the Commons from its MPs.

At local level LEAS consult in varying measure the local branches of the teachers' unions and many have teachers' consultative committees on which representatives of the unions sit. Education committees include representatives of teachers' unions or the consultative committee. Local branches and county associations have lobbied local authorities for increased spending in their schools and been involved in drawing up plans to go comprehensive. The unions also joined with the Association of Education Committees and the Society of Education Officers to argue the case successfully for education committees being a statutory requirement in local authorities after their reorganization in April 1974.

In the more general business of shaping public opinion the unions also have a vital role. They, more than any other organizations, have the resources and the staff to research and develop policies independent of the Government, and are able to present complete facts and figures on their proposals. The unions attempt to create a climate of opinion which can assist the DES and Secretary of State in securing sufficient resources for education. They also present evidence to commissions such as the James Inquiry into teacher training. When its report appears they comment, as they did on the James Report and thus contributed to the Government's proposals to implement it published in the 1972 White Paper. Then by commenting on the White Paper they influenced what actually happened.

On topics of school curriculum and examinations the unions exert their influence through the Schools Council. This was established in 1963 by the Conservative Minister of Education, Sir Edward Boyle, following combined pressure from the representatives of the NUT and LEAS. It includes representatives of LEAS and unions. It sponsors research projects on curriculum developments on numerous topics from reading to maths to environmental studies to classics, science, PE and more. It has also investigated new examinations for sixteen-plus and for the sixth forms, these exams to be run by separate boards under its aegis.

Thus the range of subjects covered by the teacher unions is wide. The NUT Easter conference in 1972 supported motions on the salary claim, on not registering under the Industrial Relations Act, on an interim report on teacher participation, on criticism of the James Report, on condemnation of large classes, on the need for expansion of pre-school education, on working conditions in schools, on support for comprehensives, on teachers' pensions, on the need for professional unity and on the need for more expenditure on education. Its 1972 annual report included also actions on museum admission charges, the lack of new secondary school building, co-operation with the British Association of the Control of Aircraft Noise, school meals supervision, support for the NUS on proposals for union finance, in-service training and many other professional and educational matters.

3 Problems

The unions, in particular the NUT, have an important role in the education service both in shaping public opinion and in the detailed working out of policies. Consulting them both for their opinions and technical information is an essential part of government in education. The unions build up proposals in a way that the DES – with the constraints of not wishing to act controversially – and the smaller pressure groups – without the resources – are less likely to. Thus the unions are important in the development of the service and, particularly the NUT, have had considerable success in having their policies adopted, albeit in a modified form. After the strikes of 1969–70 the Secretary of State, Edward Short, appealed in a speech at the NUT conference that, despite the bitterness of the strike actions, the union should help 'rebuild this triangle of confidence and co-operation' with DES and LEAs. How, he asked, could he bear a grudge against his old friends in the union.

The unions are as pressure groups and professional bodies identified with the education service. The policies and concerns of the NUT provide a guide to the coming things in education, to the kind of progress which the service anticipates. At its 1972 conference there was the reassertion of comprehensive schools, demands for the withdrawal of Circular 8/60 and the expansion of nursery education, pressure for more resources, concessions on teacher participation, whilst behind the scenes there was discussion of problems of social disadvantage and of more flexible exams, Schools Council proposals on more relevant and broader curricula and developments in similar

33

directions. In the NUT 1972 presidential address by Mr H. Allison there was the timely expression of wider social concern:

> [The teacher] performs a vital service to the community. If he succeeds the future prosperity and happiness of the nation is assured. If he only partially succeeds – or fails – uncertainty, greed, unchecked ambition, industrial, racial and religious strife threaten the future.

Two other features of the identification with the education service are the emphasis on the need for more resources and a rejection of party politics in education. Certain kinds of controversy are seen as devaluing current education and discrediting the education service. For example, as we shall see in chapter 8, the General Secretary of the NUT lumped deschoolers and freeschoolers in with those like the NAS who aroused concern for violence in schools and with right-wingers who wished only to harm the public education service. In a study of the NUT, a prominent member of it, Dr Walter Roy, wrote:[4]

> There is a firm stand against party political involvement, and an attitude of keeping out of party politics at all costs, based partly on the teacher's conception of his job [his professional status], partly on his instinct of self-preservation at a time of encroachment by the major parties on the educational service, and partly on the recognition that the greatest danger to professional unity comes from . . . alignment with party political groups.

One problem therefore is concerned with the increasing militancy. When the union's members march in support of their pay claim, shouting 'Thatcher OUT OUT OUT', it interferes with the union's ability to present a respectable, responsible, politically neutral image to the Secretary of State. The successes of the unions in educational policy have depended upon the combination of responsibility and technical information which, first, is difficult to reconcile with militant action in other spheres and, second, has not succeeded for the unions in pay negotiations. The amount of money available for teachers' salaries came under increasing inspection and control from the Government during the 1960s and early 1970s, and thus good relations with the DES were of less importance than impact nationally.

Governments appeared to exploit those unions which were respectable and did not push their case to the point of disruption.

Different sections within unions have interpreted this problem differently. The executives and leaderships, except in the NAS, have maintained their respectability in order to maintain their educational influence and agreed only reluctantly to more militant action. Younger teachers and, in the NUT, the Rank and File, have argued that militant action was not only necessary on pay but that stronger union action was required on other topics in order not so much to come to an agreement with central government and local authorities as to force their hand. It would also encourage the self-respect of teachers themselves. Faced with this threat both to their status as responsible lobbyists and as leaders of the union, it can easily happen that union executives devote more energy to attempting to control their own dissidents than to representing the union. It easily happens that union leaders are in the position of defending Government policy to the membership, and the real division of opinion is not between Government and union, or employers and union, but between union leadership and union militants. Dr Roy's study reported that:[5]

> There are times when the small, but well-organized minority of communist teachers are a worry to the leadership, but on the whole, there is no serious problem of infiltration; indeed, the picture that has emerged shows determined and successful resistance to such infiltration, and to attempts to bring the Union into the orbit of party political activities.

Dr Roy's book was published in 1968. The president of the union elected for 1973–4 was a communist, Mr Max Morris, but by then the problem was not communists. The dissidents were the more radical left, International Socialists, International Marxists and others with no specific allegiances.

In 1968 a handful of teachers dissatisfied with the moderate line of the NUT in the pay negotiations and identifying themselves with the rank and file of the union formed themselves into a group to be called Rank and File. They began publishing a magazine of the same name and this has become a medium for radical criticisms of the union and of education generally. The group formed on the issue of salaries and took the credit for encouraging the NUT to introduce strike action and other demonstrations into its tactics. Its members also found common ideas on education, rejecting the authoritarian role in which teachers were placed (not only in terms of discipline but also of education as the teacher initiating the child) and the concept of professionalism. Rank and File has proposed that schools should be democratic with governing bodies of parents, teachers and pupils and with elected executive officers in place of headteachers. A statement agreed in July 1969 included the argument:

> Exams, selection, competition and authoritarianism help perpetuate the entire social structure. A few are prepared for positions of privilege and control, while the many are taught not to criticize their circumstances.

By the beginning of 1973 Rank and File claimed 1,000 members in over forty local groups and a circulation for *Rank and File* magazine of 10,000. It is not therefore a large group but one with influence through its magazine and through its activities within the union.

There was, however, another reaction to the increasing militancy, that is against it, and a few thousand teachers broke away from the NUT to set up a separate association, reasserting the concept of professionalism. The Professional Association of Teachers held its inaugural meeting in September 1970, the nucleus being teachers who objected to the NUT's strike notices and compulsory levy. One small group of them put an advertisement in *The Times Educational Supplement* and from there its membership snowballed to over 5,000 at the beginning of 1973 and to supporting an office in Derby. Having objected to striking and to the leftwards movement in the NUT as out of keeping with the concept of teachers as professionals, the members of PAT also found common ideas on education. They were concerned at the damage done to the children both directly by losing school through the strikes and by the bad example teachers were setting. Likewise, they saw their educational ideas as founded in a concern for children and in representing the views of the classroom teachers. From a different political position they, too, were concerned at the form of leadership dominating the NUT.

There is another set of problems. Ronald Manzer[6] concludes his study on the power the NUT wields:

> The National Union of Teachers must now be regarded as a powerful conservative influence in the politics of English

education. This conservatism is explained by the Union's traditional professional concern for the education of the individual, its refusal to sacrifice longstanding educational ideals, the distractions created by divisions inside the teaching profession, and the threat to the collective role of teachers in the policy-making process posed by a more national orientation and centralization of educational policy.

The effect of this, he says, and of the uncertainty of the Department of Education in asserting society interest in education has been a 'muddling through'.

The problem therefore posed by the way in which the teacher unions are involved in the processes of consultation is that in their position of great influence they may be, first, representing teachers rather than education and, second, limiting the framework of ideas available for discussion. Teachers' interests in education are in the education which they practise, which is perhaps the education we have rather than the education we need.

References

1 R. D. Coates, *Teachers' Unions and Interest Group Politics*, Cambridge University Press, 1972.
2 M. Kogan, *The Politics of Education*, Penguin, Harmondsworth, 1971.
3 R. A. Manzer, *Teachers and Politics*, Manchester University Press, 1970.
4 W. Roy, *The Teachers' Union*, Schoolmaster Publishing Company, London, 1968, p. 130.
5 Ibid., p. 115.
6 Manzer, op. cit., p. 158.

4 Pressure groups

1 Arrival

The growth of groups to put pressure for a particular point of view or to represent the interests of its members was a phenomenon of the 1960s in all areas of social policy. Tenants' associations, amenity societies, environmental groups, claimants' unions and on the national scene Shelter, all with varying degrees of noise, militancy, efficiency and orderliness put their case before the public and before public authorities. In education likewise a small number of national associations and a much larger number of local groups have formed. For the most part they have not been in any sense militant, though rows over the 11-plus have roused demonstrations in some localities. Some groups have been concerned primarily to press one point of view, some to propose reforms across the spectrum of educational policy-making and some have been more concerned to provide a service for their own members. A common cause to many of these groups, however, is the right of parents to representation.

These pressure groups or interest groups have now become a part of the educational scene. In a few local authorities the local group of the parents' body, the Confederation for the Advancement of State Education, or the parent–teacher association may be asked for or present its opinions on a frequent and friendly basis, although they are not involved in regular consultations as are the teachers' associations. Generally these groups are established to operate in this kind of way, joining in the consultations and presenting evidence, gathering and spreading information. Compared to local groups operating, for example, on planning decisions, they tend to be more orderly, though the arguments in the Inner London Education Authority about transfer of children at eleven included capturing ILEA members and a ritual chaining of protesters to the railings of County Hall. Their actions are generally constrained by the education system and its highly institutionalized nature. In education there are, furthermore, few specific incidents on which to demand immediate action, and the groups tend, when they are involved in the politics of the system, to look for longer-term outcomes and for ways of working within the system.

The growth of parental organization is often expressed, particularly from the Conservative side, in terms of consumerism. Parents have less opportunity to choose and pay on the free market and therefore demand their 'consumer protection' in another form. Sir Geoffrey Howe, at the time of writing minister responsible for consumer affairs in the Conservative Government, expressed this in 1969 (*Caseviews*, 4, CASE, 1971):

> If Directors of Limited Companies are required, for the protection of prospective investors, to publish full and accurate information about their affairs, why should schools that are often near-monopoly suppliers be expected to do less? If those who offer package holiday trips – as well as independent school proprietors – are rightly subject to the provision of the Trade Descriptions Act, why should local education authorities be allowed to go on publishing inadequately generalized 'guides' to the nature of their schools? In an age when consumer protection is rightly required in so many fields, parents should be given enough detailed and accurate information to enable them to choose between different comprehensive schools.

It may be expressed in educational terms. There has been, prompted particularly by the Plowden Report (see chapters 6 and 10), an increasing appreciation by teachers and educationalists of the value of closer relations with parents, and this has assisted the establishment of PTAs and the recognition of other groups. Sir Edward Boyle, when minister of education in 1963, spoke of parents as the 'fourth partner' in the education service alongside central government, local authorities and teachers. Amongst some parents' groups there is a more socialist or Labour Party commitment to state education and to its improvement. The Confederation for the Advancement of State Education, whilst it is a non-party organization, summed up these two points (*Caseviews*, 4, CASE, 1971):

> Our pressure for greater recognition of the parents' role is in part derived from a belief that interested parents are a positive advantage to the children's education. It also in part stems from a belief that the citizens in a democracy should

participate as fully as possible in government decisions, and that this is especially applicable in relation to educational decisions and parents.

This statement from CASE goes on to point out that 'membership of a political party should not be a prerequisite for participation', and this suggests another factor contributing to the growth of pressure groups. The major political parties have been unable, partly because of the range of issues they must cover and partly because of their preoccupation with the problems of government, to develop a policy on many specific issues. Thus pressure and interest groups are formed and put their case to whichever party is more appropriate, or often direct to the relevant government department. It may sometimes be more useful to tackle the party in power or it may be better to persuade the opposition to attack the Government on behalf of a group or interest. In local government the tactical situation is often similar, and something like this may be appropriate for small groups of teachers with regard to the teacher unions.

Membership of pressure groups, particularly the parents' group, is very much a middle-class affair, although individual associations may have conscientiously broadened their base. The groups also tend to be dependent on the enthusiasm and dedication of a fairly small number of people. A local group is likely to start as a handful of friends or colleagues from another association and to survive and have an impact does not need to actively involve a great many people. People who run pressure groups usually reckon that less than half a dozen activists are needed but they need to be able to spend several hours a week, often on mundane tasks. They also need, until the group is very established, a considerable rapport among themselves. This is true of local groups, even though there are parents' groups with upwards of a hundred members in a locality. It is also true that national associations depend upon, perhaps, one, two or three people making its organization almost a full-time job.

Most groups locally have been formed to act on one issue, usually comprehensive reorganization or fund-raising for a school. As such there is always the likelihood that when the incident or need has passed, the group will disband, but in practice many keep going by spreading their field of interest. Local groups which have formed to promote comprehensive reorganization have, for example, become associations of CASE and run programmes of speakers and discussion groups on educational issues. If the immediate interest passes and if the handful of activists move from the district or give up, then the group may fold, but even if some individual groups are ephemeral the phenomenon is lasting.

2 Pressure, information and support

The first function of many of these groups is to put pressure on central and local government to further their particular views on certain issues. Sometimes the group may turn its attention to persuading other bodies such as the teacher unions. It will seek to do this by presenting arguments to the individuals and offices most concerned and, less directly, by gathering public support. The group may have as its target MPs, councillors, civil servants, education officers, headteachers or a less precise area of public opinion. It will aim for them both directly and through newspapers, magazines, television and radio. It may tackle a particular subject as a group by itself or win allies among other groups.

Different tactics will be appropriate depending upon the objects of the pressure but there is no general way of defining this: even though the aims are the same, tactics might need to be different for different groups and different issues. For the most part, however, the group uses the fairly obvious ways of arousing attention and putting arguments. First a group may seek general publicity through national or local papers, then it may write letters or present petitions or organize meetings with MPs, civil servants, councillors or education officers. It may organize public meetings both as an expression of opinion and to spread its point of view. It may organize demonstrations or some form of direct action, and may lobby MPs.

All these activities are intended to make its case heard and be considered; and sometimes by the strength of support to force or to chivvy central or local government into incorporating the group's ideas into their policy. Whichever tactics are used it is also important to attract public notice, and for this much may depend upon the press coverage of them.

Such activities do not, however, appear to be the major element in the work of the pressure groups, particularly in the longer established ones. The main job comes to be the gathering and supply of information. The group needs to argue its case supported by the facts and technical information. To be effective a group needs to make this information available in the pressure activities to its members generally and to the press. Dr W. D. Wall, Vice-President of the National Confederation of Parent–Teacher Associations, told its annual conference in London in 1970 (*Parent–Teacher*, NCPTA, Autumn 1970):

> We can be an intelligent, articulate pressure group; that is to say, we want, we know what we want, and we know why we want it. We have all the arguments. We have to recognize that participation at any level, whether it is an attempt at getting a sensible national decision on an educational issue or whether it is an attempt to improve the resources, staffing, the methods of a school, that participation in decision-making implies an obligation to know, to find out, to instruct, to understand the differences in roles according to who you are and what your precise relationship with the school is.

Bodies like CASE, STOPP and the Campaign for Comprehensive Education place a strong emphasis on the collection of information and its dissemination. The last, as we shall see, has taken on the role of propagating information which would assist both those making the case for going comprehensive and those local authorities who wanted to draw on the experience of others in using different kinds of schemes. One might have expected the DES to have done this, just as many local CASE groups have produced booklets of basic information about schools to make up for lack of information published by the LEA.

Thus, as well as needing information to argue particular proposals, the group comes to have the function also of supplying useful information to its members. It is, in fact, hard to overestimate the need for information about education, particularly about what is available in different schools or about the procedures for putting one's view to the education office and teachers. Local authorities, though much improved, have a tradition of regarding most information as automatically confidential. Parents bewildered by the processes of schooling, particularly as their child nears school-age and nears transfer to middle or secondary school, often have to turn to information produced by voluntary groups.

Pressure and interest groups come to exist partly to support their own members – with information and with comradeship. Organized groups help individuals both in having their opinion presented to, say, the local authority and in, say, making contacts with school and teachers. Officers of groups tend to put offering advice and information high on the list of tasks they undertake.

Some groups were actually started to provide support rather than pressure, but the different functions become intertwined. A group which is brought into existence for some kind of mutual self-help, perhaps for people affected by a specific handicap, tends to be led into the more political pressure functions. It does so partly because of the frustrations of trying to improve the lot of a minority without changing aspects of the administrative and political framework. It does so also because its expertise in the subject is often required by other bodies, commissions or departmental investigations. It may have to make representations on behalf of its members' interests and is drawn as a body into the processes of consultation and of working towards a consensus.

3 Groups at work

The several dozen pressure and interest groups include associations formed to help children with particular handicaps,[1] associations of teachers of various subjects and associations to promote certain developments in education. This section looks at the operation of the major groups concerned with parent participation and allied causes, with educational issues of general interest and with the campaign for increased pre-school education.

Confederation for the Advancement of State Education

CASE is primarily a parent group, a confederation of about 105 local associations with national and institutional members. It described itself thus: 'We are mostly engaged in white-collar occupations in the South of England, and include a fair sprinkling of school teachers, further education lecturers, and other people professionally connected with education' (*Caseviews*, 4, CASE, 1971). It has probably about 10,000 members though an exact figure is impossible to tell as husbands and wives may share membership and as membership is first to the local association which passes on *per capita* subscriptions. Thus, as it says itself, it cannot claim to represent all parents but it does claim to represent the right of parents to be represented.

The association began in Cambridge in 1960 when a group of parents got together in dissatisfaction at facilities in their primary school and, having investigated the situation, discovered their school was considered to be better off than others. They drew up these objectives for the association:[2]

1. To obtain and spread information about all educational facilities provided by the State;
2. To work for the improvement and enlargement of State educational facilities;
3. To improve communication between local education authorities and all interested in education, and parents in particular.

Publicity in the press about the activities of the Cambridge group encouraged the formation of groups in other areas, so that in 1962 a joint committee of them was formed and in 1963 the first annual conference was held.

The predominant issues for CASE are the right of parents to be represented and the need to open up schools to their communities. It has recommended that school governors and managers should include representatives of parents and that independent tribunals or ombudsmen be appointed to arbitrate between parents and local authorities, particularly in matters relating to choice of schools. It has demanded that all LEAs should produce annual reports and make public the agenda and minutes of their meetings.

Its interests and opinions are promoted on a much wider range of issues. At its annual conferences and in the evidence it presented to the Labour Government for a New Education Act CASE has made recommendations ranging from opposition to corporal punishment and compulsory religious education in schools to changes in industrial training and adult education. As a national body it is pro-comprehensive and deplored Mrs Thatcher's Circular 10/70, and though among some local associations there have been doubters and opponents of particular comprehensive schemes, all support the idea of comprehensive reorganization.

At national level policy is made by an annual conference, and the organization kept going by a committee which meets half a dozen times a year and a great deal of voluntary work by its national secretary and other officers. Locally an association for state education may consist of just a handful of friends or up to 500 people, most groups being about a hundred or less. It would most likely have been started by a small group of middle-class parents dissatisfied with arrangements for 11-plus selection or perhaps with nursery provision. The national secretary sends out kits containing advice on how to set up a group. It would be based on a local authority rather than one particular school. Like all voluntary organizations it might depend upon the work and enthusiasm of one or two people, and some local groups have collapsed when these people have moved or lost interest.

Certain local associations, such as in Reading, have played a large part in persuading their authority to go comprehensive by lobbying councillors, publicizing their arguments in the local press and even by drawing up a proposed scheme of reorganization to put to the education committee. Where more forceful action has been needed on comprehensive reorganization the local CASE group has often co-operated in a special campaign, a STEP group (Stop The Eleven Plus), rather than get too embroiled in the battle itself.

Nationally and locally CASE tends to be an orderly organization, progressive but non-party and, particularly nationally, identified as the major representative of parents' rights. It places a great deal of importance on the collection and communication of information, both to encourage more progressive ideas and to advise parents. It has in co-operation with the NCPTA, through the Home and School Council, published dozens of information sheets and booklets of advice and findings. It has sent deputations to all ministers of education since 1963 and the invitation to send a member to sit on the Plowden Committee was a landmark. It has also made representations to the NUT about the union's unfavourable attitude to parents coming into school to hear children read and given evidence to the Schools Council on curriculum. It also gave evidence to the Plowden, Maud and public schools commissions and to other educational inquiries.

Locally associations have arranged meetings on subjects as various as sex education, open-plan schools, methods of collecting dinner

money, children's rights and the gifted child and have made representations to local authorities about comprehensive schools, road
safety at a primary school and parent participation. Others have
organized 'education shops' where advice is offered. Some, like
Basildon, have prepared handbooks on the local provision and
facilities of schools. Some have run study groups for more detailed
discussion on issues like middle schools or provision for handicapped children.

The Sheffield Association for Education, one of the long-standing
groups, looked back over its first ten years in 1972 and concluded
that on most of the issues on which it has pressed the local authority
has agreed with it. It pointed to parent representatives on all governing and managing bodies, to the publication of information about
schools, to improved facilities in schools, for example, for music
education, to comprehensive reorganization and to community
facilities on school campuses. This has been a very fruitful though
admittedly individual situation because of there being a co-operative
education office with a secure Labour council and a strong local
association with the national secretary, Mrs Barbara Bullivant,
among its members.

National Education Association

The NEA has as its motto 'Preserve the best: improve the rest'. Like
CASE it presses for greater attention to be paid to parents' wishes but,
where CASE is more progressive, the NEA is more concerned with
established standards and with freedom of choice rather than
representation.

The NEA – an entirely different organization from the United
States teachers' association of the same name – claims 35,000
members in local branches, affiliated associations and individual
memberships. Its members include schools and teachers as well as
parents. Its history goes back to 1965 when a group of parents
brought a successful action in the courts against the introduction of
comprehensive schools in Enfield. They discovered other groups
attempting to save the grammar schools in Richmond and elsewhere
and joined forces. The NEA went on to co-ordinate campaigns to
save grammar schools in many parts of England, notably Surrey and
Buckinghamshire.

The objectives of the NEA include:

To preserve what is best in and to further the development of all types of secondary schools so that full provision is made for the needs of boys and girls according to their abilities and aptitudes.

To support the principle that parents should have real freedom of choice between different types of school to the greatest possible extent, and to this end to work for the retention of schools of proved worth.

The association does not reject comprehensive schools as such. It believes that grammar schools and their established standards should be maintained and that comprehensive schemes fail to provide the variety of provision for ability and aptitude described in the Education Act 1944.

The NEA sees a decline in educational standards and, according to a resolution passed at its annual conference in May 1971, 'views with concern some of the recent curriculum changes, doubtful methods of teaching and the excessive freedoms thrust upon the immature, and calls upon teachers to examine with courage the mistakes which are being made'. Its concern for standards is applied also to its rejection of teacher-controlled CSE exams and its defence of external GCE exams. Its conference in 1971 also proposed that sex education should be an extra-curricula subject taught only upon the written request of the parent.

The NEA is concerned, as are similar organizations, at the difficulties of parents in being heard. It is concerned at the public being kept out of the parts of the procedures under Section 13 of the Education Act 1944 dealing with the LEA's response to the DES on local objections. Its main concern is that parents are given less freedom in choosing their children's schools, and it has proposed that parents should be provided with vouchers which they would spend on schools of their choice (chapter 8).

But as well as the promotion of its policies and the publication of leaflets discussing them and associated ideas, a great deal of the work of the NEA is on individual cases. Its Honorary General Secretary, Mrs Ruth Bradbury, a leader of the original group in Enfield, has parents ring up and ask for advice or assistance. The NEA is often able to support parents in their protests to LEAs, particularly over transfer to secondary schools, with the legal and political knowledge its officers have built up. An individual parent might lack the information, skills or strength to carry through his case but a national association or local branch can provide the support.

National Confederation of Parent–Teacher Associations

The NCPTA owes its existence to a conference called by the Birmingham Federation of PTAS in 1954. Parent–teacher associations had been formed in a number of schools during the late 1940s and early 1950s, many of them grouping into regional federations. It was thought to be time for a national organization. The NCPTA had 1,200 affiliated associations at the beginning of 1973.

The NCPTA regards itself as a service organization rather than a pressure group in any political sense. Local PTAS are more likely to be concerned with their individual schools and school facilities than with national education policy. The NCPTA has national policies which it publicizes and puts to government departments but they are more concerned with welfare and facilities. At the 1972 annual conference the motions passed agreed with Okehampton School PTA that there should be a campaign against the exploitation of sex in advertising, with the Friends of Wellsway School, Keynsham, Bristol, that first aid facilities were often inadequate in schools and with Cheshire Federation of PTAS that LEAS should provide social and recreational facilities for children between eight and thirteen. Other motions expressed disapproval of the ending of free milk and called for parent representation on managing and governing bodies. Rather than exert pressure, as CASE does, the national confederation may take up issues presented by individual PTAS, for example on the school not getting the new buildings it needed or on half-price admission to football matches up to the age of sixteen.

Within the NCPTA there is a suspicion of politicking and pressure group activities. It holds a delicate position in these times of increasing demands for parent participation in keeping parent and teacher interests together, and it has representatives of the teacher unions on its executive. Its main purpose, as is that of the individual PTA, is to keep people in touch with each other. The NCPTA provides, with CASE and the Home and School Council, many working papers, information sheets and booklets. It advises on setting up new PTAS, offers an insurance scheme and deals with a formidable number of inquiries and requests for advice on practical matters.

The establishment of a PTA in a school depends upon the head-teacher. The idea may come from parents or teachers but it would not be able to be set up unless the headteacher accepted it. Some PTAs are not affiliated to the NCPTA, largely, it is believed, because their headteachers do not want them linked to a national organization.

The strength of PTAs is simply in making contacts between school and home. They need the national confederation for contacts and advice rather than for political cohesion. A lot of local activities centre around fund-raising for the school. PTAs all over the country have collected cash for swimming pools or for adventure play-grounds, televisions and other special equipment. Activities include wine and cheese parties and car rallies, sponsored walks and jumble sales as well as discussion of educational issues and the more serious side of home and school co-operation.

Advisory Centre for Education

ACE is not a pressure group as such but a professionally run advice centre for the use of whose services one has to pay. It is, however, involved in much the same work as the parents' pressure groups and has the same kind of commitment to the parent cause, although it has approached these functions from a different angle. Whereas pressure groups have been formed to argue a case and have then developed information services, ACE was founded to provide information and has therefore been taken into arguing for the rights of parents and pointing out the need for certain reforms.

ACE, which is registered as an educational charity, was established in 1960 as a consumers' organization for education, an attempt to repeat the achievements of the Consumers' Association in education. Its aim therefore was to provide the information and advice which would help parents become better users of the education service and to raise their consciousness of being consumers. ACE provides information and advice through its monthly magazine, *Where*, and by answering inquiries from subscribers to the magazine – its members – and non-subscribers on payment of a fee. It was cal-culated that the advisory service received 100,000 letters asking for advice between 1960 and 1970, but these, ACE realized, represented only one part – and a mainly middle-class part – of the need for information. One of its most important contributions to making information more widely available was in pioneering 'education shops' which, often in a section of a large department store, gave information to inquirers over the counter. Education shops have since been run by parents' groups, the educational priority area projects and local education authorities.

However, simply in gathering information and supplying it, ACE was involved in a struggle for parents and itself to have this information. It has worked to change the climate and to have the rights and importance of parent involvement recognized, and in this was performing a pressure group function with its lobbying and publishing. ACE's director, Brian Jackson, in one of its series of occasional papers, *1960–1970: A Progress Report*, referred to ACE as a 'maverick', 'idea-spinning, risk-taking, straddling the disciplines, unafraid of existing power, pressure, and yesterday's ideas'. ACE has been a dynamic and big enough organization not only to exert pressure but to undertake schemes such as setting up the National Extension College, a pilot body for further education by broadcasting and correspondence, helping the *Sunday Times* set up a technical college places clearing-house, picking up the Liverpool Educational Priority Area project and helping maintain it as a centre for action research into urban community education – the director of the Liverpool EPA project became co-director of ACE – and spotlighting many other gaps in national and local provision.

Home and School Council

The Home and School Council is a co-operative venture of CASE, NCPTA and ACE, and is administered by them jointly. It now acts as a medium of communication between the three bodies and as a publisher of jointly produced booklets. Its list of publications includes working papers on *Parent/teacher relations in secondary schools*, *How to be a school manager or governor* and *Handbook for parents with a handicapped child* and information sheets on a variety of topics including school counsellors, examinations, parents' rights and religious education.

The Home and School Council is much less than it was originally intended to be. Established in 1967 it was inspired by a vision of one great association representing and linking parents and teachers. It was a vision largely of ACE's Chairman, Michael Young, and Director, Brian Jackson. There was a hope that CASE and the NCPTA would be able to dissolve their identities into one body, but rivalry and suspicion that ACE was empire-building combined with the different interest of parent and teacher associations to wreck the idea. The teacher interests in the NCPTA were not only offended at implied criticism from parents and from the permanent office which the Home and School Council maintained for a couple of years, but also rejected the idea of a strong parent-based pressure group. The grant which had been raised to set up the organization ran out. The story provides a number of lessons: different pressure groups have different interests; teachers were suspicious of parent participation; and, on the positive side, the council had a continuing value as a source of information, if not opinions.

Since the Home and School Council deflated, there have been a few attempts to revive the vision. Brian Jackson wrote in the *Home and School Newsletter* (September 1971): 'What we badly need in the next decade is a National Union of Parents and Pupils which will be party to decisions affecting their interests, as the teachers are party to ones affecting theirs.' It would be formed out of ACE, CASE and the NCPTA. He was writing in support of an article proposing a parents' union which would take its place beside the teacher unions in national debate and consultations about educational policy. The next issue of the newsletter was to have contained a report of reactions to this proposal, but, after it had been printed, certain people in the parent–teacher movement were so offended by some remarks slighting them that the whole article had to be torn out before the newsletter was distributed. Such is the politics of pressure groups.

National Association of Governors and Managers

NAGM was formed in 1970, as it describes itself, 'to be a link between governors and managers and to press for reforms', reforms which would 'give them a fuller role in the democratic administration of education'. It would include on governing bodies representation of parents and thus would be integrating parents' representatives into the structures of the education system. Compared to the other bodies which are concerned with more participation and parent representation, NAGM lacks a large membership and a popular base. There is a national committee which exercises some co-ordination over a few strong local branches and a number of independent members. The members are predominantly governors and managers.

NAGM has confined itself to the specific cause of governors and managers and has a careful and detailed policy both on how the present system could be improved and what reforms should be introduced in a new Education Act. It argues that the need for greater parent participation and the need under the larger local authorities after reorganization for a more local expression of interests could be met by strengthening governors and managers. For the present it demands that there should be parent representation on managing and governing bodies and that the bodies should be made more effective by ending party political appointments to them, allowing them discretion in the allocation of school budgets and involving them in staff appointments. Under a new Education Act it would seek to have managing and governing bodies consist of equal numbers of parents elected by parents, teachers elected by teachers and members appointed by the local authority. They would have defined powers over expenditure. NAGM sees managing and governing bodies as a means of reconciling the interests of teachers – and of their professional independence and academic freedom – and of the public; they would be a means of self-government for the school and of fostering communications between parents and staff.

NAGM has put its case, as have the other pressure groups, through publicity in national and educational press and has taken a deputation to the DES. Its annual conferences have so far been primarily concerned with formulating the policies described above. Its local groups have in a few authorities put their case successfully and managing and governing bodies have been reformed, as in Sheffield. It has not, however, carried its arguments into new localities as much as built on interest which was there already or on a willingness by an LEA to hear its case.

Campaign for Comprehensive Education

The Comprehensive Schools Committee was formed in 1965. Its first purpose has been to collect information about comprehensive schools, simply to supply correct information in place of the prejudices about comprehensive schools, believing that this in itself together with assisting local groups and local authorities was sufficient to prove the case for comprehensive schools. Later it established a permanent office with paid assistance in London. It publishes a journal and collects the most complete information available on progress with comprehensive schemes in all local education authorities. It changed its name to Campaign for Comprehensive Education in 1970 after the election of the Conservative Government in order to widen the campaign to include middle schools and all forms of education in the sixteen to nineteen age-group. It sought also to follow through comprehensive reform inside the schools themselves.

The Campaign is an organization of teachers and educationists rather than parents. It is non-party and has included prominent Conservative supporters of comprehensive schools.

The CSC has developed much further than other groups into a professional organization and has too the most developed research and information services. Mrs Caroline Benn has been responsible for collecting detailed information on comprehensive schemes and for authorship with Professor Brian Simon of two reports in 1970 and 1972, *Half Way There*.[3] Local groups seeking to argue for comprehensive schools have drawn on its knowledge but so too have LEAS in formulating schemes and wanting to draw on the experience of others. In doing so, and in its information services generally, it was really providing a back-up service to Government policy, one which the DES did not provide.

Throughout the Labour Government arguments for comprehensives were becoming irresistible. In this context the CSC had less to argue the case than to hurry the process along by displaying the advantages of comprehensive schools by arranging visits and through spreading facts and figures. It organized conferences for local groups on tactics, supplied speakers and published leaflets. Central Government was exercising political pressure with varying force upon local authorities. The CSC was accepted as the authoritative body on the subject, trusted by many local authorities.

The Campaign for Comprehensive Education continues with these activities but the Conservative Government has thrown the argument about comprehensive schools back to local authorities. The Government does nothing to encourage, in some cases discourages, comprehensive schemes, and local authorities have to work out their own futures individually. In this context it is groups like STEP or local CASE groups which have been the more appropriate organizations to work through. The national campaign can support local groups with advice, information and co-ordination but there is less it can do to bring pressure at a national level. Under the Conservative Government with Mrs Thatcher as Secretary of State, its main task was to mount a campaign against a 'co-existence' policy of comprehensive and grammar schools in favour of full reform.

Society of Teachers Opposed to Physical Punishment

STOPP was formed in 1968 by a group of young teachers and it is deliberately controlled by teachers, even though amongst its six to seven hundred members there are parents and other interested people. In many ways STOPP is a classic pressure group, besides having an appropriate name. It has one particular aim – the abolition of corporal punishment in schools in England and Wales – which is regarded there as radical. Just as it has not diversified its aims, so too it is still run by the same small group of people who started it, London-based as an organization but with supporters all over the country. As a minority it saw it would be more effective as a body working in, but separate from, the unions. Most of its members are NUT supporters but the union itself has many other preoccupations and is opposed to this cause.

STOPP aims to abolish corporal punishment in schools either by act of parliament or, in the nearer and more realistic future, persuading LEAs to end the practice in their areas. To do this it needs not only the politicians' but the teachers' support. It lobbies, campaigns, writes circular letters to local authorities and issues press statements. In 1972 two sets of circular letters were sent out to local authorities and to MPs; both were largely aimed at discovering people who supported their cause and who could join them in persuading others. Local education committees in most cases 'noted' the letter, or passed it on to the teachers' consultative committee, or rejected it. STOPP's hope was that even so certain councillors would respond individually and contact them. Likewise STOPP officers watch the press for likeminded and possibly influential people who can be contacted.

A joint campaign with the National Council for Civil Liberties in the autumn 1972, was geared to the publication of a Penguin book edited by Peter Newell, *A Last Resort?*,[4] which argued the case and presented research on the abolition of corporal punishment. Letters were written by STOPP and Peter Newell to MPs and chairmen of education committees asking for support. The publication of the book and the letters were reported by newspapers and broadcasting media, gaining the support of *The Times Educational Supplement*. In 1973 Baroness Wootton intended to introduce a bill in the House of Lords to abolish corporal punishment, not in the hope of getting it passed but at least to gain publicity.

The success of a campaign is hard to judge. Some favourable replies to letters are received, though the majority fail to get any response. New supporters are found, and presumably a few people are persuaded by the arguments put forward. Replies from LEAs are rather more valuable because of the information they provide about corporal punishment in their area. Gradually, through such means and through lobbying individuals and organizations, there have been specific moves against corporal punishment. The ILEA banned it from primary schools in 1972. Shropshire announced that, as a result of the STOPP campaign and pressure by local teachers' associations, infants would no longer be caned. Certain London branches of the NUT began to oppose it, and the Young Teachers NUT conference decided to reconsider the issue. The NUT itself remained immovable, arguing that corporal punishment was a professional matter for individual teachers and a necessary last resort.

It is interesting that these things are achieved without militant action, and that, as with the parents' associations, a premium is put upon information both to use in the campaign and to assist local members who may be pressing or querying some action of their own local authority. Results of research and replies from local authorities are circulated to members. This quiet approach by STOPP is in part a tactical approach to the particular issue: shouting would have raised tensions on what is an extraordinarily emotive subject, which would have worked against STOPP. In part it is a tactical approach given the nature of the education system: a sudden breakthrough is unlikely because the system is highly institutionalized with power diffused among many bodies and there is a weighty consensus to shift.

National Campaign for Nursery Education

The success story of pressure groups in recent years has been the lobby for increased pre-school education. The National Campaign for Nursery Education spearheaded this, helping to exploit the evidence of research and the popular mood. It has organized, lobbied, presented petitions and captured newspaper headlines with demonstrations by mothers and small children. The expansion of nursery places in the White Paper published in December 1972 was marked up as a success for the campaign.

The Campaign for Nursery Education was formed in 1965 by people and organizations of all political parties and of many different interests. Its executive committee included representatives of the Save the Children Fund, Pre-School Playgroups Association, Nursery Schools Association, National Union of Teachers, Transport and General Workers Union, the Health Visitors Association and the Business and Professional Women's Clubs, among others. The objective was clear: 'to press for increased provision of educational and play facilities for children under five' and, more specifically, to campaign for the lifting of the restrictions imposed by the DES in Circular 8/60 against expansion of nursery education. The emphasis was on nursery schools and nursery classes, but playgroups, even with possibly divergent aims, were included in the campaign. During the period of the campaign there was a great wave of research evidence showing the importance of the early years of childhood in learning and the social deprivation suffered by many children at this crucial stage of their lives. The Plowden Report in 1967 brought the issues into focus.

The campaign, based entirely on the labour of volunteers, achieved some remarkable publicity *coups* and mass demonstrations of popular support. On 21 May 1968 1,500 people and a 'lollipop parade' of under-fives lobbied the House of Commons and presented a petition of over 98,000 signatures to the Secretary of State for Education, Mr Edward Short. Two months later Mr Short announced that the urban aid programme would include nursery places in the priority areas. Local groups, including those in Birmingham and Paisley, also organized petitions supported by marches of mothers and toddlers. They raised funds, lobbied their local councillors and held public meetings, although the main effort had to be national as the local authorities were restricted by Circular 8/60. On 2 May 1972 a petition of 365,000 signatures was presented to Mrs Margaret Thatcher as Secretary of State and was accompanied by a day of photogenic and headline-catching demonstrations by mothers and children. Soon after that it became clear that

Mrs Thatcher was going to introduce plans for expanding nursery education, and these were part of the White Paper in December.

The Nursery School Association

In the pre-school movement two other main bodies worked in and beside the National Campaign for Nursery Education, they being the Nursery School Association (known as the British Association for Early Childhood Education from January 1974) and the Pre-School Playgroups Association. The NSA is the professional organization for the schools and their teachers and was established in 1923. It has 6,000 members, including parents and other interested people as well as teachers, college lecturers and nursery nurses, who are organized in local branches and into a national organization through fifteen area committees. Its concern is particularly for high standards in staffing, building and organization of nursery schools and classes. As the professional association for nursery schools and teachers, it is consulted by the DES. It provides information and opinions on nursery schools to central government and may brief MPs before debates in the House of Commons, as well as being available to press and broadcasting requests for information. It has a permanent office with paid secretarial assistance and much voluntary work. A great deal of its daily work, as with other associations, is answering questions and offering advice to parents and public who write in, and this as much as deputations to ministers or public meetings is the part required of it in the education system. It also publishes leaflets and through its research committee acts as a catalyst for research into nursery schools.

Pre-School Playgroups Association

The Pre-School Playgroups Association illustrates the potential of voluntary movements, the growth from one mother's initiative in 1961 – when she formed a group where her child could play – into ten years later a national organization co-ordinating a vital part of the country's educational provision. The PPA identified a need, an alternative form of pre-school education at a time of restriction on nursery places, a form which would have to depend on the mothers themselves. As it developed, it became clear that playgroups were not just a temporary expedient, a second-best to nursery schools, but

LPP—E

had virtues in themselves. Although the PPA worked actively under the umbrella of the nursery schools campaign and shared its sense of success at the White Paper in 1972, its interests were always potentially divergent.

The development of the PPA was assisted by grants from the DES which allowed it in 1966 to appoint a national adviser and in 1970 another, as well as by grants from charitable bodies. It has had an office and some full-time staff for nearly ten years but was further helped by a grant from the Department of Health and Social Security in 1972. At national level it is mainly concerned, as well as campaigning for the cause, with exercising some control over developments and building up the quality of the movement. It is the 260 local branches which work with the actual playgroups, helping them start or running them, co-operating with local authority playgroup advisers, if any, and channelling grants from LEA or local social services departments to groups.

The success of the PPA, apart from its hard work and campaigning, lies partly in having identified the need for a voluntary preschool education and having provided a convenient vehicle for central and local government support. The DES and local authorities could offset some of the disadvantages of statutory restrictions on nursery places by supporting or helping fund voluntary movements. The value of playgroups, however, is not just to the children but to the mothers who help run them and to the communities in which they are situated. Thus the playgroup movement has been associated also with the growing realization through the 1960s of the importance of home background and the consequences of social deprivation. It has also tackled the problems not in the traditional way of the education service, that is by removing the children, but by working with mothers and children together. The mothers have gained by finding out more of how children learn and by developing their own social skills. The out-and-out supporters of nursery schools claim that only teachers and nursery schools or classes can provide the standards and professional expertise which children need, but the playgroup movement argues that other values can be as important as professional standards, among them community involvement and the socially beneficial effects of helping people to help themselves.

References

1 J. Stone and F. Taylor, *Handbook for Parents with a Handicapped Child*, Home and School Council, 1972.
2 *This is CASE*, Home and School Council, 1972, p. 1.
3 C. Benn and B. Simon, *Half Way There*, McGraw-Hill, London, 1970; revised edn, Penguin, Harmondsworth, 1972.
4 P. Newell (ed.), *A Last Resort?*, Penguin, Harmondsworth, 1972.

5 Authority and experts

1 The headteacher as an autocrat

The chapters so far have described the distribution of powers and duties in education and have constructed a system in which a number of bodies interact in the process of consultation and negotiation, policy-making and administration. This chapter considers the actual running of the schools by headteachers and LEAS. The way in which the schools are run seeks to avoid political controversy, and yet its basis and its consequences are political in effect.

Responsibility for the schools is vested in the LEA, the board of managers or governors and the headteacher, but if one talks to headteachers or local government officers about these formal mechanisms of power there is often an ironic reaction, a slight curl of the lips, which implies that the real power is otherwise. The real power, it implies, is a matter of personalities, of those personalities who do the real work.

The individuals who have the day-to-day powers of running the schools and education service do, in a curious way, not answer to democratic bodies, certainly not in the manner of theoretical concepts of political masters and plodding, obedient bureaucrats who implement their decisions. Schools are run by headteachers who have assumed the responsibilities vested in more public bodies and they have done this not out of unscrupulous craving for power but because that is the role which the headteacher is expected to carry out. Local education offices are frequently dominated by officers to the extent that any elected members who want to have influence have to identify themselves with the officers' concerns. There is therefore a problem of how schools as public institutions are in practice accountable to the public. In what ways are schools responsive to public demands?

The prelude to any such discussion is the sign near the school-gate which reads 'Parents may not go beyond this point'. It has acquired almost legendary status in writing about education for its encapsulation of the idea that parents and schools should be kept apart, that parents are an impediment to the education of children. Signs like this are reported to be coming down as PTAs and other links between home and school are formed. The experience of parents or members of the public who try to influence the running of schools is still, however, often uncomfortable and frustrating. The administration of the education service appears to be solid and monolithic from the outside, but the member of the public who has found a way inside discovers that there it is even more confusing. The diffusion of power within the education system through the checks and balances and by the informality of its processes makes it difficult to find where decisions are made and who takes responsibility for them. This has a profound effect on the kind of actions possible by parents and other outside pressure groups and upon the way in which any responses are made to their demands. Complaints and protests have to take account not only of the formal powers and responsibilities in the system but also the assumptions of the people working in the service.

The formal statements of school management are contained in the rules of management for primary schools and the articles of government for secondary schools. Each school must have, according to the Education Act 1944, a board of managers or governors; in some local authorities a board supervises all or a number of the schools and in other authorities each school has its own. The boards consist of a mixture which varies from LEA to LEA of local councillors, members of local political parties interested in education and other local dignitaries or residents appointed by the LEA. The rules of management or articles of government divide the responsibility for the schools between the LEA, the board and the headteacher. The LEA is usually given responsibility for determining the general character of the school and the place in its educational system. The board of managers or governors is given the responsibility for the 'general direction of the conduct and curriculum of the school' in consultation with the headteacher. The headteacher is given responsibilities for the 'internal organization, management and discipline of the school', for the choice of equipment, books and teaching methods and for the supervision of staff. The actual wordings vary.

The headteacher is therefore given the powers to run the school. The responsibilities of LEA and managers or governors overlap with that of the headteacher, and it could be said that in curriculum and school organization the 'general direction' of the governors is a stronger power than that of the headteacher. Different local authorities and different boards of governors make different demands of their headteachers but by and large he is left in control and most managerial powers are in practice exercised by him. Considering how other powers are diffused in the school system the individual power of the headteacher is remarkable. Indeed, such are the assumptions made about his role, as Anne Corbett observed writing in *New Society* (15 April 1971), that within the schools '"benevolent dictator" or "liberal autocrat" is seen as a term of praise'.

The LEA usually believes in letting the headteachers get on with the job of running the school. It gives him considerable managerial responsibilities for supplies and equipment, and the tendency is for schools to be made more independent with the consequence that the headteacher gains in power. Schools are increasingly given annual budgets based on capitation allowances for books and equipment so that they can decide how best to spend the money on the teaching they are doing, and the headteacher therefore has more decisions to take and more sanctions than when the education office supervised the spending of every penny.

One of the factors in the role of headteachers is therefore the educational and managerial efficiency of devolving such responsibilities to the schools, but related to this are other factors. In teaching the decisions about content and methods are made by teachers themselves. They are reckoned to be the professionals and the experts who know how best to do the job. They are also reckoned to have a right to a certain academic freedom, a concept which is involved with both the concept of the professionalism of teachers and the need to protect education from political interference (chapter 3). The authority devolved to headteachers is in part an embodiment of this trust placed in teachers. There is also in English education a deep-rooted suspicion of standardization, and this also is often involved with the concept of academic freedom in being associated with fears of state control.

The headteacher runs the school. Sir Alec Clegg, Chief Education Officer for the West Riding, giving a lecture to the child care staff of the National Children's Home in June 1972, put the truth starkly:

Every education officer of a large authority knows perfectly well that there are schools in his area to which he would not under any circumstances, send one of his own children. As we all know, the most frequent cause of a poor school is the quality of the head. He may be ill or weak or lazy or incompetent, but unless his failing is gross it is difficult to relieve him of his post.

The headteacher has the power, partly because of the responsibilities devolved to him and the school by the LEA and partly because of his autocratic role in the school. He has managerial powers on supplies and equipment and a formal statement of curriculum responsibilities in the articles of government. The headteacher has, moreover, security of tenure: if he decides to stay in a job, it is almost impossible to fire him, unless he commits an offence or grossly neglects his duties. For a local authority to interfere with the headteacher's responsibilities would probably be construed as creeping totalitarianism or as bureaucracy getting above itself. The headteacher's position is also strong with regard to the staff of the school. The teachers have security of tenure, but they depend upon the headteacher for appointment to posts of responsibility (and the extra pay which goes with them). They also depend upon headteachers for references when they apply for other jobs. They may depend upon his decisions for a fair share of teaching the subjects and classes they would prefer – this usually means not teaching the thickies and not teaching religious education, such is the relationship between morals and expediency.

The headteacher is, however, expected to consult his staff, and he will probably prefer to gain the consent of his teachers for his actions. He will, however, probably believe that the actual decision has to be his; as a guard against seeming to favour certain individual teachers, against politicking among the staff and as a means of maintaining his authority. The Head Masters Association (HMA), in a statement in October 1972 which was taken as a change of heart in favour of more teacher and parent participation in the running of the school, still made it clear that the final authority of the head was to be untrammelled:[1]

> The opinion of the staff is a factor in almost every situation which a headmaster is required to assess and needs to be taken into account before he reaches a decision. Sometimes, by giving

his colleagues information or offering them a reasoned argument, he will be able to change their views, but he will hardly ever be in a position to ignore them.

Some recent developments have modified the powers of head-teachers. One is the factor of size; with the establishment of comprehensive schools of well over a thousand students a managerial organization has to be developed simply because the headteacher cannot cope with everything. Teachers may be put in charge of houses, or years, or upper and lower schools, and this is to give the children a greater sense of identity as well as for managerial reasons. The introduction of management techniques through a limited amount of training which is provided for headteachers has also contributed concepts of delegation of responsibilities to those who are actually doing the job.

There have, too, in keeping with other changes in social thinking, been doubts cast on the propriety of having one man in charge for life. In January 1971 the Conservative MP, Mr Timothy Raison, put a private member's bill to parliament which proposed that heads should be appointed on a renewable contract of a limited number of years, arguments which were opposed by the NUT. But disillusion with the absolute power of headteachers has been growing more generally for several years. In January 1968 at the conference of the Assistant Masters Association, usually reckoned a more conservative union, the retiring chairman, Mr L. Curry, looked forward to the time when a school could be run by a small elected body of experienced teachers. It was, he said, too much of a gamble under the present system of appointments to put one man into such a position of power and influence as head of a large school: 'It is time that we devised some better system than this relic of Victorian individualism.' Chapter 9 discusses demands for more participatory structures.

The power of headteachers has also been modified by the growth of boards of governors and managers. Governing bodies have traditionally been ineffectual, gathering for tea or sherry in the headteacher's office once a term and putting in an appearance on prize-giving or sports day, and making no contribution beyond the sheer honour of their presence. However, demands for greater involvement of the community and for the devolution of managerial responsibility have encouraged a reassessment of governing bodies.

The reorganization of local government for 1974 produced larger local authorities, and governing bodies have been seen as a means of maintaining a local community interest. They have also provided a means of teacher- and, in a few authorities, student-representation. The DES has encouraged LEAs to reconstitute governing bodies for individual schools. The NAGM has argued that governing bodies should be strengthened, given defined spending and made more representative of the community.

The autocratic position of the headteacher survives, however, and is rigorously defended. The HMA in its statement on *The Government of Schools* in 1972 commented on proposals for greater participation:[2]

> Our most fundamental objection to the determination of school policy in educational matters by majority vote of the staff is that such a concept involves an implicit denial of the existence, or at least the importance, of a genuine profession of teaching.

It argued that at the bedside of a sick man a surgeon, rather than a ballot of junior doctors, had the 'experience, knowledge, skill and judgment' to make decisions and that the headteacher's job in schools required similar 'expertise'. Schools required the 'coherent leadership' of headteachers:

> Because a headmaster's standing is dependent upon the well-being of his school and because his independence makes it unnecessary for him to court popularity, he is in a position to make disinterested decisions on educational grounds. In many schools, good relationships with parents . . . rest upon their faith that the headmaster's authority will be exercised with judgment, integrity and dedication to the welfare of his pupils.

The headmaster could also be an innovator whereas new ideas might be resisted if the majority of staff had to approve them. The headmaster could also provide continuity in the school whereas staff turnover 'could cause chaos if school policies were at the mercy of every fluctuation of common room opinion'.

The HMA has provided a definition of the best of an autocratic role. The role is not a product just of formal statements of responsibility – the LEA or governors could, if politically skilful, exercise their constraints – but of the assumptions about it. The headteacher is expected to be a leader. The convention is that the headteacher has the last word and exerts his authority in the crunch. And, the headteacher might say, he is the poor sod who has to carry the can if anything goes wrong; he bears the white man's burden. A survey by Anne Chisholm in *The Times Educational Supplement* (29 September 1972) showed that the image of the headteacher as patriarch is strong:

> Most heads are proving remarkably tenacious in hanging on to both their status and educational values – not, on the whole, because they are reactionary or authoritarian, but because they hold deep convictions about what society expects of them. . . . The ideals that inspire them are still primarily of the old-fashioned, Arnold type, stressing responsibility, public service and above all a belief in the virtues of self-control.

Frank Musgrove[3] has argued for the solitary status of heads: 'The headmaster will find the gratifications of office at the golf clubs and the Rotarians. On the school premises he must accept loneliness and learn to turn it to good account.'

The headteacher is expected to be a leader; it is 'his school'. Headteachers do not like to think of themselves as 'mere administrators' or managers but as educational, and moral, leaders. He takes responsibility and apportions blame and praise within the school. Society seems to expect this role, berating individuals for failings of institutions. A headteacher may feel he has to build himself up to this position; it is lonely at the top. The system of DES and LEA administration devolves a lot of responsibility upon the school, and it is the headteacher who embodies the school.

Headteachers are therefore very concerned to maintain their responsibility and when criticized, possibly even in headlines in the local press, may feel the criticism personally. It becomes a criticism not just of the school but of him, the correctness of his action, and his whole sense of responsibility. In relationships with outside bodies and with parents and PTAs the head has to maintain his position. He may need to prove that he knows best, and in discussions and consultations he is likely to feel that it is his duty to take the decision himself. One effect of this is that once a headteacher is seriously challenged on one issue, then the whole personality and interrelated sets of values and actions is threatened. When authority is made so personal, the challenge on one decision very easily changes into a challenge to the whole nature of authority in the school.

2 The administration as force

Nothing is simple in the education system. As we have found in previous chapters, the complexity and the imprecision of the relationships between regulations and advice has an effect in itself. Much of the educational administration exists in a world of shadows and hints. In many ways this produces a desirable situation and assists adapting to a consensus rather than to controversial change, to steady progress rather than a dramatic combination of innovation and false starts. But it also delays change, reduces the ability of people to influence what happens, and reduces the ability of the system to implement its own decisions.

Nowhere is this complexity more real than in the local education office. The position of the LEA *vis-à-vis* the central government was dealt with in chapter 2, and *vis-à-vis* the headteacher in the previous section of this chapter, but now we must turn to the LEA itself and to the education office.

The chief education officer or director of education is the head of the section of the local authority offices dealing with education. He is responsible to the education committee, a committee of the council, and as such one might interpret his role as that of a bureaucrat who simply implements the decisions which the committee passes down to him. This is far from the actual situation. The experience of those involved and the research undertaken in this area show that the chief education officer can be just as significant and powerful as the committee, possibly more so.

In a study of Cheshire, J. M. Lee found that the permanent officials were the main force because the issues and tasks were too complicated and far-reaching for representatives with limited time at their disposal to undertake:[4]

> It is misleading to think of the county council primarily as a body of elected representatives who make decisions of policy and then order officials to execute them. . . . It is better to regard the system of county government as a body of professional people, placed together in a large office at county hall, who can call upon the services of representatives from all places throughout the area which they administer.

In fact, as Lee goes on to point out, some of the elected representatives 'by sheer ability and drive make themselves indispensable to the successful working of the machine'. And D. Peschek and J. Brand, who studied the West Ham and Reading authorities, found the power shared between the CEO and a few crucial elected members.[5]

Officers may be suspicious or exceedingly cautious about the education committee and its political manœuvrings, but those who within the service are counted as good officers are also likely to manipulate the committee. There is also a feeling of comradeship in the education service and identity of purpose in which officers and elected representatives work together. In the national organization of the Association of Education Committees, for example, both officers and elected members take part and are represented.

A study of the ways in which two county boroughs, Gateshead and Darlington, decided to go comprehensive by Richard Batley, Oswald O'Brien and Henry Parris[6] concluded that 'politician and administrator work in partnership' and showed that the roles had been different in the two boroughs. In Darlington the plan of comprehensive schools which was adopted, after debate and consultations, was that of the CEO and was known as the Peter Plan after him:[7]

> Perhaps the most important development . . . was the apparent
> conversion of the Chief Education Officer to the comprehensive
> principle. He was aware that, in the changing climate of
> opinion, and given the likelihood of Labour returning to power
> both locally and nationally, comprehensive education would
> come, and that it was his duty as a good administrator to be
> prepared. In any case it was becoming necessary to re-examine
> the development of secondary education for practical reasons.

In Gateshead the education office and key members of the Labour Group collaborated in preparing the draft proposals but the plan itself left certain options open. The CEO played a crucial role in working out the implications of the plan and filling in the technical details, in consulting with the teachers' associations and in presenting solutions.

The CEO is in the most crucial position in the administration of education. It is he who sorts out conflicting demands made by different interest groups and who manages the processes of consultation. It is he who is best placed to step carefully through the complexity of regulations and pressures on the operation of the education system, both because of his power as head of the office, partner of the education committee and expert status and because of the qualities expected of the CEO. There is a romantic tradition of the great CEOs as leaders of educational thought, civilized and civilizing, idealists and administrators, men who could interpret the real interests of parents and children.

Derek Birley, formerly Deputy Education Officer of Liverpool, in describing the job of the CEO, wrote of the quality of 'concern' needed:[8]

> There is no process in educational administration that can be done completely satisfactorily unless those with responsibility for it care deeply about the fundamental purposes of the service. . . . Serving the community is not just an added attraction for the education officer to provide. It is not something to be grafted onto his work; it must permeate his whole approach.

It is this humane quality one finds most often in CEOs. They, just as headteachers, are inspired by an Arnold, though perhaps son Matthew, poet and school inspector, rather than the patriarchal Dr Arnold, headmaster of Rugby School, and by a concept of serving and educating the community. This is seen as a subtle, almost spiritual, process which is not susceptible to the hurly-burly of committee and pressure group politics.

Edward Britton, general secretary of the NUT, writing in the local authorities' magazine, *Education* (17 September 1971), observed that the role of the CEOs in the 1970s would be less romantic than it had been in the past:

> The CEO today has less opportunity for panache, and, if he appears directly in the public eye, it is more likely to be as a defender of his committee than as a leader of educational thought. Those who hanker after the romantic view see in this a change for the worse. Others see it as inevitable. Absolute monarchs are more romantic than constitutional kings and queens; dictators are more romantic than parliamentary prime ministers, but there comes a time in human affairs when the issues are too important to be left in the hands of one individual.

The situation of the CEO has been affected also by the increasing acceptance of ideas from management sciences and the introduction of policy committees in local authorities. Some of their individual pre-eminence has been lost in becoming one of several chief officers under a county chief executive and in the increasing importance attached to the heads of social services departments. But these moves have not changed the styles in which they combine the roles of administrator and educator nor their roles in the complex pressures of the education service.

3 The spirit of the service

Individuals and pressure groups usually find difficulty in directing a complaint or trying to influence schools and education offices. There is a guardedness against the public, which tends to be so whether the public is Jonathan Parent or the education committee. What are the elements in the service which produce this?

The section on headteachers quoted a common argument against greater participation: You wouldn't tell a surgeon how to operate, so why should you tell a schoolteacher how to teach. As this glib thought indicates, the teacher, like the surgeon, is an expert and a professional at his job: he has been taught to teach and has qualified through examinations to do so; he has status and expert knowledge; and he is a member of a body of colleagues. There is in education a professional dedication by teachers and officers (who are former teachers) which is expressed in the belief that they know what is best. As experts in an expert service, they know better than laymen what is required, what are the best teaching methods and the real nature of children. They are likely to have a conviction that their judgment should take precedence over committee and other political decisions.

The general attitude of those in the education service is that they are making progress steadily and, in some ways, going in advance of public opinion, which is feared to be reactionary. Thus a group which forces an issue and raises a hue and cry is thought to threaten progress. It might be thought that they are acting on false or inadequate information. It might be thought that they have precipitated a crisis or exposed the nature of the progress before people were ready to accept it. A fuss is presumed to set the clock back.

(It seems to be a general assumption that time and progress move in the same direction.)

Such professional attitudes include the belief that progress is more likely to come from individual leadership rather than from group decision-making. Individuals are thought to be more efficient and more able to judge truly between competing claims than committees with their various vested interests, as the HMA statement quoted in the earlier section showed. Likewise arrangements are better made informally rather than formally, by person-to-person contact than in a committee or in public.

Committees and pressure groups are thus suspect not only for making problems but also for supposedly representing only those people who shout the loudest. The administrator finds his judgment is a better guide to what is really needed than is public opinion. He may seek to devalue public pressure in order – depending on political attitude – to protect either the silent majority, the quiet, respectable middle classes, or the inarticulate, the underprivileged who lack the middle-class skills of communication and organization. The dedicated professional thinks of himself as fair and able to avoid self-interest in a way in which representatives of localities or particular interests are not.

Derek Birley, in describing how to deal with parents in comprehensive reorganization, expressed this mistrust of the public and reliance on professional judgment:[9]

> It would be surprising if the public were not taking a lively interest in all this, particularly if there is disagreement. How can the LEA keep them informed, reassure them and take account of their views? Very few of the public are likely to be well-informed on the educational issues; concern for their children tends to colour their views; sheer weight of numbers precludes anything but the most superficial discussion of the issues.

He proposed public meetings and keeping heads informed so that they in turn could inform parents and 'help to answer their queries and allay their fears'. The political basis of this part of the school system does, in summary, rest upon the acceptability of individual authority, a belief in professional dedication and academic freedom, and a concept of civilizing people. One effect is that the system does not respond directly to demands for change. Those working in the education service prefer to assimilate demands and pressures into their overall concept of steady progress rather than to respond to specific demands. The system is adapted by incorporating new ideas, ideally keeping pace with what is perceived as the movement of the consensus.

The difficulty is that when there are demands for specific changes, changes which may be the implementation of an agreed central or local government policy, the system is no readier to respond than it would be to extreme demands of a particular pressure group. The process of assimilation, slow, unspecific response combined with the decentralization makes for conservatism and the maintenance of the *status quo*. It also makes for frustration for those who attempt to tackle the system.

A further problem is the private nature of the system and that when there is cause for public discussion it is difficult to organize and even more difficult to use as part of a decision-making machinery. The reliance on individuals combined with the informal processes of the system produces an under-the-counter operation. One of the effects of this is that the public are forced into protest rather than participation in rational debate. It has sometimes in the past seemed as though to form a pressure group or protest movement could be counterproductive in that it might draw attention and publicity which would arouse antagonism, whereas the change could have occurred anyway as part of the normal progress.

A substantial challenge to this style of operation was presented in the early years of the 1970s when there were increasingly vocal and organized protests from parents, often prompted by the re-organization of secondary schools. There were also more articulate demands from the political left and right that schools should be made more responsive to parents, ratepayers and their elected representatives.

In *Socialism and Education* (1972), the journal of the Socialist Educational Association, Councillor Sinclair Lewis of Norwich proposed that under a new Education Act, LEAs should lay down the broad outlines of syllabuses: 'At the moment local education authorities have very little control over the schools they administer. They have no control over the curriculum, the ways things are taught, the attitudes created in schools, the atmosphere of the school.' The problem he was tackling was that councils who had introduced comprehensive schemes had to rely on teachers being sympathetic and the objectives of the comprehensive reform could be frustrated by autonomy given schools and teachers.

From a different political direction there were the ideas of the Black Paper writers and supporters of the National Council for Educational Standards. Its chairman, Dr Rhodes Boyson, a comprehensive school headmaster and a Conservative parliamentary candidate, declared in a speech to its annual conference in January 1973 that parents would cease to send their children to schools whose values they rejected and teaching efficiency they suspected. He demanded greater accountability of the schools to parents, including the possibility of headteachers being reappointed by a ballot among parents.

Those to left and right of the consensus of the education service have suspected the professional domination and demanded greater accountability. The system finds it difficult to cope with criticism, but decisions about education are related to the nature of society, and there come times when they are no longer appropriate to experts. The public debate on values and assumptions should override them, but the service is not thoroughly democratic. It has elected bodies but those headteachers and officers with the most functional power are deliberately protected from their influence. The service is tolerant, civilized and largely humane, but it assumes that it knows best, and shields itself from public involvement. There are fundamental arguments about the kind of authority which schools and the education service have and about the way decisions are made. The most substantial shift in recent educational debate is this challenge to the values of the system.

References

1 *The Government of Schools*, HMA, 1972, p. 18.
2 Ibid., p. 7.
3 F. Musgrove, *Patterns of Power and Authority in English Education*, Methuen, London, 1971, p. 119.
4 J. M. Lee, *Social Leaders and Public Persons*, Oxford University Press, London, 1963, p. 214.
5 D. Peschek and J. Brand, *Policies and Politics in Secondary Education – Case Studies in West Ham and Reading*, Greater London Papers No. 11, London School of Economics, 1966.
6 R. Batley, O. O'Brien and H. Parris, *Going Comprehensive*, Routledge & Kegan Paul, London, 1970.

7 Ibid., p. 7.
8 D. Birley, *The Education Officer and his World*, Routledge & Kegan Paul, London, 1970, pp. 105 and 188.
9 Ibid., p. 99.

Part two

Education for social change

Part two

Education for social change

6 Equality of opportunity

1 Secondary education for all

Education is not something apart from society; it is not, on the whole, something done for its own sake. The central thesis of social concern from the late nineteenth into the twentieth century has been that through improving the education of children, one would be able to produce both more intelligent adults and a more just society. The means chosen has been to provide more school, college and university education and thereby to broaden the opportunities of children to partake of this education. The result, no matter how cynical or doubting one is about education, cannot be denied: there is a lot more of it about.

The great expression of this social concern has been for 'equality of opportunity'. The theme of 'equality of opportunity' has been interpreted differently. In recent years it has been identified with the arguments for comprehensive schools, but in this it has to undo what was earlier proposed in its name, namely the 11-plus and the differentiation of grammar schools and secondary moderns. In the 1960s this issue brought together politicians of all parties, and when Conservative minister, Edward Boyle, agreed with future Labour minister, Anthony Crosland, on 'equal opportunity of acquiring intelligence' the consensus was perfect. The pursuit of the ideal in the late 1960s and early 1970s turned to pre-school education, and school-based solutions seemed increasingly inadequate. The development of the theme 'equality of opportunity' represents the story of education through the century.

What exactly the phrase 'equality of opportunity' means is not clear. Roughly it implies a fair start in life, an opportunity for all children to develop their faculties and to proceed into adult life and employment without being adversely affected by poor homes and families. But, to use the metaphor of a running race, 'equality of opportunity' can mean variously the opportunity to start together, the opportunity to benefit from staggered starts, the opportunity to finish together – and sometimes no more than the opportunity to run on the same track. Arguments have shifted ground, involving at different times different ideas of educational ability and social justice and different concepts of the ways in which ability can be measured and exploited. The two main strands of the theme – educational and social – are interwoven so that at various times and in various arguments one or the other takes precedence: in terms of education it can mean the provision of equal facilities and attention and in social terms it can mean the use of education to achieve a more equal society. Disillusion with the ability of education by itself to make for a more equal society has led to a concentration upon ways in which society can be made more equal in order to encourage more equality of opportunity in education.

The nineteenth century laid the foundations of the present school system, the main concerns being to keep children out of factories and to provide an elementary education. The Education Act 1870 and subsequent legislation established a system of compulsory, universal elementary education run by the local school boards and by the church bodies. Secondary education developed separately, run by private bodies, the churches and the local authorities, so that in the early years of this century there were two distinct types of school education. Elementary schools were free and took children to the ages of twelve or thirteen, whereas the secondary schools were fee-paying, took children to the age of sixteen and beyond and were largely the preserve of the middle classes. Opportunity for the working classes was extended by offering a proportion of free places at secondary schools by a scholarship exam. This proportion had been fixed in 1907 at 25 per cent of secondary places but many children were unable to take up these places because of family circumstances. The Annual Report of the Board of Education in 1911 found that not more than 5 per cent of elementary school pupils progressed to secondary schools.

The nation went to war in 1914 and returned, as seems to be its habit, to a major education act. As the Liberal President of the Board of Education, Mr H. A. L. Fisher, observed in introducing the bill in the House of Commons:[1]

> When you get conscription, when you get a state of affairs
> under which the poor are asked to pour out their blood and to
> be mulcted in the high cost of living for large international

policies, then every just mind begins to realize that the same logic which leads us to desire an extension of the franchise points also to an extension of education.

There was, he believed, a growing sense that industrial workers were entitled to be considered fit subjects for any form of education from which they were capable of profiting. Industrial workers themselves wanted education not only to become better technical workers and earn higher wages, but 'because they know that in the treasures of the mind they can find an aid to good citizenship, a source of pure enjoyment and a refuge from the necessary hardships of a life spent in the midst of clanging machinery in our hideous cities of toil'. It was scarcely radical thinking but the Education Act 1918 pulled the education system together and gave all children free education (in elementary schools) until the age of fourteen.

The infant Labour Party, as Rodney Barker describes,[2] played an undistinguished role in the debate, succeeding only in having provision for some post-school delayed. Within the Labour Party at this time there were, Barker says, conflicting views on education, which have their parallels today. The Fabian view, as articulated by Sidney and Beatrice Webb, was élitist and meritocratic rather than egalitarian. Sidney Webb wrote in *The Basis and Policy of Socialism* that 'every clever child in every part of the country shall get the best possible training'.[3] He therefore encouraged the scholarship system and referred to secondary schools as 'the greatest capacity catching machine that the world has ever yet seen'. A different, more egalitarian, more democratic socialist view was that attention should be paid to improving the elementary schools of the majority of the population and to providing a freely available education up to university level. Barker quotes a warning by J. A. Hobson on the scholarship system:[4]

> You will find that this selective process, if it is allowed to be made the substitute for the higher education of the people, will simply take certain individuals and put them through a class machine, in order that they might become effective guardians of the vested interests of the possessing classes of this country.

As the Labour Party moved towards and into power the principal plank of its policy was 'secondary education for all', which as a concept fell short of radical ideas and which in practice – the grammar school and secondary modern system of post-1944 – was élitist. 'Secondary education for all' was propounded by R. H. Tawney in a pamphlet of that name published in 1922. In forming the basis of the party's policy for the next thirty years, it was, as Barker says, 'an almost perfect illustration of the character of the Labour Party'. It drew on ideals of social equality but its proposals only sought to make the existing system more available.

The Labour Party's policy was given currency and legitimacy by the report of the Hadow Committee, *The Education of the Adolescent*.[5] It advocated that the education system be established into two parts: 'primary' and 'secondary'. 'Primary' would take children up to the age of eleven, whereas 'elementary' included beyond eleven for those children who did not achieve scholarships into secondary schools.

The Hadow Report identified two phenomena. The first was adolescence, which is taken for granted nowadays, but it is worth the effort to recall Hadow's prose:[6]

> There is a tide which begins to rise in the veins of youth at the age of eleven or twelve. It is called by the name of adolescence. If that tide can be taken at the flood, and a new voyage begun in the strength and along the flow of its current, we think that it will 'move on to fortune'.

The second was that during this time of life children had different aptitudes and abilities. This concept was potentially democratic in recognizing that pupils should have the opportunity of secondary education but that not all required the same form. For some, said Hadow, the traditional academic grammar school education was appropriate, and to this end existing secondary schools should be renamed grammar schools. For others a more 'realistic' type of education was appropriate in which studies would be 'related more closely to the living texture of industrial and commercial or rural life'. It would be 'designed to stimulate interest in boys and girls who are beginning to think of the coming years and a career in life, and are likely to feel the liveliest quickening of the mind when they see the bearing of their studies on that career'; for these the secondary modern schools were appropriate. For yet a third group technical schools would be appropriate.

The Hadow Report chose eleven as the age of transfer from

primary to secondary schools in one of those convenient solutions where both existing administrative arrangements and theory coincide. Transfer at eleven fitted both with the system of scholarship selection and with the start of adolescence. At eleven it would be possible to define the interests and the aptitudes of pupils, the committee was advised, and psychological tests would be available to take an exact measure of these different abilities. That test was to be known later as the '11-plus', and it was justified by a metaphor: 'the most pleasant of parks will . . . have an entrance and an exit'.

It took nearly twenty years to implement the Hadow Report in the Education Act 1944. During the intervening years various half-cock measures were introduced to extend opportunity by increasing the number of scholarship places, by raising maintenance allowances and by tentatively and ineffectually raising the school leaving age to fifteen. Two further reports confirmed the main lines of Hadow. The Spens Report in 1939[7] and the Norwood Report in 1943[8] hardened proposals for a tripartite system of grammar, technical and secondary modern schools and for assessments of ability and aptitude using IQ tests. The Education Act 1944 took the arguments that different abilities and aptitudes required different forms of education and formed a school system.

2 The issues

From our perspective the Education Act 1944 was the great breakthrough, setting up the school system we know today. It formed one system for all children, bringing together elementary and secondary schools. At secondary level it brought the existing secondary and the old senior elementary schools together under one code and it abolished fee-paying – and the ability to buy one's child's secondary education in the state system. It established larger, stronger local authorities, gave the minister for education powers to supervise and co-ordinate nationally and brought church and state systems together. It made clear once and for all that there was a state system of education, rather than state intervention and support for a voluntary service.

But there had been, as the previous section of this chapter shows, a long haul up to the act, and in its time it could be seen rather more as a consolidating measure. The concept of education as a 'continuous process' went back to the Labour Party's Tawney Report in 1922 and the foundations of the act were in the Hadow Report. The Labour Party had in and out of office during that period attempted to prompt the reforms which the 1944 Act was to legislate. The times were right; people's thoughts were turning from the war and the chances of losing it to the victory, the peace and the reconstruction. The war had had its political effect upon education, fostering not only a communal spirit and a need for optimism about the future but also showing the nation to itself; one of the causes of national concern about education was the evacuee children from the cities who had presented such a surprisingly deprived picture to the countryside into which they went.

The White Paper on Educational Reconstruction (1943) introduced the purpose of the new measures:[9]

> To secure for children a happier childhood and a better start
> in life; to ensure a fuller measure of education and opportunity
> for young people and to provide means for all of developing the
> various talents with which they are endowed. . . . The new
> educational opportunities must not, therefore, be of a single
> pattern. It is just as important to achieve diversity as it is to
> ensure equality of educational opportunity.

Educational psychologists had provided the justification in the Spens Report:[10]

> Intellectual development during childhood appears to progress
> as if it were governed by a single central factor, usually known
> as 'general intelligence', which may be broadly described as
> innate, all-round intellectual ability. It appears to enter into
> everything which the child attempts to think, or say, or do. . . .
> Our psychological witnesses assured us that it can be measured
> approximately by means of intelligence tests. . . . We were
> informed that, with few exceptions, it is possible at a very
> early age to predict with some degree of accuracy the ultimate
> level of a child's intellectual powers. . . . Since the ratio of each
> child's mental age to his chronological age remains
> approximately the same, while his chronological age increases,
> the mental differences between one child and another will

grow larger and will reach a maximum during adolescence.
... Different children from the age of 11, if justice is to be
done to their varying capacities, require types of education
varying in certain important respects.

The Hadow, Spens and Norwood reports discovered the idea that
the same kind of education was not appropriate for everybody, but
the White Paper's idea of how children should be selected at eleven
had a much rosier view of the process than the practice which was to
follow: 'On an assessment of their individual aptitudes largely by
such means as school records, *supplemented if necessary by intelligence
tests* [my italics], due regard being had to their parents' wishes, and
the careers they have in mind.' The Norwood Report had described
the new feature on the educational landscape:[11]

The pupil in this group (for realistic or modern studies) deals
more easily with concrete things than with ideas. He may have
much ability, but it will be in the realm of facts. He is interested
in things as they are. ... His mind must turn its knowledge or
its curiosity to immediate test; and his test is essentially
practical. ... Because he is interested only in the moment he
may be incapable of a long series of connected steps; relevance
to present concerns is the only way of awakening interest,
abstractions mean little to him. Thus it follows that he must
have immediate returns for his effort, and for the same reason
his career is often in his mind. His horizon is near and within
a limited area his movement is generally slow, though it may be
surprisingly rapid in seizing a particular point, or in taking
up a special line.

These are the children to whom the modern school would be appropriate. The Spens and Norwood reports had been critical of the
ability of the grammar school curriculum to cater for this pupil and
critical of the 'conservative and imitative' character of the schools:
'Perhaps the most striking feature of the new secondary schools
provided by local education authorities ... since 1902, is their
marked disinclination to deviate to any considerable extent from the
main lines of the traditional grammar school curriculum.'[12]

This discovery of the non-academic pupil and his needs could be
construed as radical and democratic. But our perspective must be
found in the Spens Report's recommendation that roughly 15 per

cent of pupils would go to grammar school. Depending, therefore, on how many go to technical school, the pupils they had just discovered comprised over three-quarters of the population. The élite has been discussing the others – and when that is how the discussion is conducted it is not surprising that progressive intentions come to little.

Comprehensive schools had been discussed. The Spens Report rejected 'multilateral' schools, comprehensives in so far as all aptitudes and abilities would be catered for under one roof. Its reasons were the same as those which persist in arguments against comprehensives: the schools would be too large (for Spens this meant 'say 800 or possibly larger', which would today be a medium-sized school); the sixth forms would be too small to make viable a variety of courses. It would also, the Spens Report believed, be difficult to find headteachers who could develop both grammar and modern curricula, so different were the philosophies.

The case for comprehensives or multilaterals was argued, however, both in the more radical areas of the Labour Party and in the TUC memorandum on 'Education After the War':

> So long as the three types of school are separately housed, the old prejudices will die hard and equality in fact will not be achieved. For this reason, and because it is valuable to the education of each type of child he should freely mix with children undergoing other types of education, it is hoped that the Board [of Education] will undertake really substantial experiments in the way of multilateral schools.

3 Comprehensive schools and party politics

When the 1944 Education Act was passed comprehensive schools were not a party political issue. In the years before the Second World War the Labour Party had concentrated upon the promotion of the scholarship and the grammar school kid, seeing in the broadening of the scholarship arrangements and improvements in support for children from poor homes the best chance of increasing opportunity in society. The implementation of the act assumed that the tripartite system of grammar, technical and modern schools corresponded to a fair assessment of mankind's different abilities and that selection was accurate.

The post-war Labour Government maintained these opinions and discouraged comprehensive schools. In 1948 it blocked a comprehensive scheme proposed by the Middlesex LEA on the grounds that the tripartite system was 'logical and usual'. Sparsely populated areas, like Anglesey and the Isle of Man, were allowed to go ahead with non-selective systems but in urban authorities they were discouraged. Coventry and London County Council were allowed to introduce a small number of comprehensive schools within a predominantly selective system but there bombing had already destroyed the grammar schools. The West Riding County Council in its development plan issued in 1948 commented that it could not agree that:[13]

> at the age of 11 children can be classified into three recognized mental types, and should be allocated to grammar, modern and technical schools accordingly; . . . that the numbers to go to each type of school should be determined by an arbitrary percentage of the age-group; . . . that at the age of 11 children show certain aptitudes which can be relied upon to indicate the type of school to which a child should be allocated.

The period between 1946 and 1964 was one of conflict in the Labour Party about comprehensives. The first ministers of education, Ellen Wilkinson and George Tomlinson, withstood demands from the floor of Labour Party conferences for multilateral or comprehensive schemes. In practice their administrative actions and guidance tended to encourage the grammar schools, as Michael Parkinson's study shows.[14] A document, *The Nation's Schools*, prepared by the caretaker Conservative Government and upheld by Ellen Wilkinson, suggested that grammar school places should be limited, that if anything there was already an excess supply. Parity of esteem, it was argued, could be created between the three branches of the tripartite system and selection for schools could now be made upon the basis of rational objective criteria, the IQ test. In 1947 *The New Secondary Education* was published maintaining the ministry's position but appearing to offer the opportunity for diversity and for experiments.

Opposition within the Labour Party to the ministry policy

strengthened. In 1948 and 1950 the conference carried motions critical of the minister's case for a tripartite system. The National Association of Labour Teachers – later to be translated into the Socialist Educational Association – said that the minister had not shown himself publicly 'even dimly aware of feeling in the Labour Party'. In the final months of the Labour Government in 1950 the minister defended himself to the Party's Home Policy Committee by arguing that the tripartite system would only be pernicious if it created a permanent segregation of manual and white-collar workers. It would be foolish to ignore the consequences of neglecting the interests of bright children which he feared might suffer in reorganization. It would be best, he concluded, to allow only limited experiment. And he introduced into the debate what was to be a rallying cry for the shilly-shally lobby: 'Because comprehensive schools are still subject of violent controversy in educational circles [they] would alienate a large vocal and influential section of opinion.' The same sentiments were to be repeated for the next twenty years.

The National Executive Council of the Labour Party, however, set up a committee to review its policy on comprehensive schools which concluded: 'The tripartite system of education does not provide equality of opportunity and is therefore out of tune with the needs of the day and the aspirations of socialism.' But the minister did not accept the memorandum, warning that the concept of comprehensive education lacked popular appeal. But by now his opinions were of small consequence, for the Labour Party was defeated at the general election. It ended its government having approved thirteen comprehensive schools, mostly in areas of scattered population, and allowed a further eight on an interim basis in London.

The thirteen years of Conservative Government which followed saw a gradual increase in the acceptance of the idea of comprehensive schools in both parties. The Labour Party moved faster, though a series of policy wrangles during the 1950s avoided out-and-out commitment to comprehensive education. In 1955 comprehensive schools were supported by the party's manifesto but the party leaders hedged. They hedged on two grounds, pragmatic and idealist. First, root-and-branch reform would not be possible given the existing structure of education. Second, they themselves were unpersuaded. For many Labour Party intellectuals the idea of the grammar school boy – in many cases themselves – held strong.

Emanuel Shinwell wrote: 'We are afraid to tackle the public schools to which wealthy people send their sons, but at the same time we are ready to throw overboard the grammar schools, which are for many working class boys the stepping-stones to universities and a useful career.'[15]

The Party doubted whether the public was as concerned about comprehensive education as it was itself. The Party's 1958 policy statement tried to get the best of both worlds by arguing that comprehensive schools would preserve the grammar school tradition: there would be 'grammar school education for all'.

However, during the years that the Conservatives were in office the large issues were thoroughly debated, and research and public opinion criticized the tripartite system. One factor was that in 1957 research reports from the National Foundation of Educational Research and the British Psychological Society found against the reliability of the 11-plus, which was the pillar of the selective system. A number of further research reports cast more doubts and criticisms. The NFER, for example, showed that 12 per cent of children were wrongly allocated. Research found that IQ was not static, that one test at eleven did not define aptitude and ability. But such attacks might not have been quite so serious if the technical and secondary modern wings of the tripartite system had lived up to the fond imaginations of Hadow, Spens and Norwood and if they had truly achieved parity of esteem with the grammar schools. First of all, in the years immediately after the war the resources were not available for enough buildings and teachers. These schools – mostly secondary moderns, for few technical schools were established – were housed in the old elementary school buildings. In keeping with the strong tradition of English education that one maintains the best and never takes away from the best in order to improve the worst, the standards of the grammar schools were maintained as a priority. The secondary modern schools suffered. They did, furthermore, with worthy exceptions, imitate grammar schools in much the same way as the Spens Report had in 1939 criticized new secondary schools for following old academic curricula. Even if one believed the psychological basis of secondary modern schools and realistic studies, one had to acknowledge that they were not delivering the goods.

There was too the experience of the public, and more particularly of the middle classes. Parents who before the Education Act 1944 might have been well-off enough to buy secondary education found that in the 11-plus their children were not only being cruelly tested but possibly failed. The numbers who could go to grammar schools varied from 10 per cent to 45 per cent in different authorities. It became accepted as common sense to see that a set of tests on one or even a few days was not a fair determinant of a child's future and no amount of special coaching or offers of new bicycles could compensate.

Other research – and this is the continuing preoccupation of most British research – provided evidence that the social class differences of grammar and modern schools were really so and not just a figment of socialists' imagination. The expansion of secondary education and its new structure were not assisting equality of opportunity. A whole string of official reports during the late 1950s and 1960s – Crowther, Newsom, Plowden, Robbins – brought home dramatically the extent of working-class disadvantages and pointed to failures of the system.

The case for comprehensives could be stated in three ways: on meritocratic grounds that society needed the most able people to prosper and that comprehensives encouraged children from all classes; on social grounds – known despisingly as 'social engineering' – that it was fair that everybody had the same opportunity and that having given it to them one was building a generally more equal society for the future; on straight educational grounds that, regardless of other consequences, comprehensives helped children to learn better. They could be described as both more efficient or socially more just, and both Conservative and Labour politicians could sympathize at some point.

The Conservative Government of 1951 to 1964, though not all sections of its party, gradually accepted comprehensive schools. As minister of education, Sir David Eccles had allowed comprehensive schools in areas of scattered population and in new centres of population so long as grammar schools were not destroyed. On the whole the party preferred to think pragmatically of comprehensives as an experiment, rather than the order of the day, and in January 1958 there were nearly fifty. The last minister of education in that government, Sir Edward Boyle, accepted comprehensives. Later as Lord Boyle, he described his policy whilst minister of education from 1962 to 1964: 'My own approach . . . had been to accept that the trend must be away from the 11-plus and towards a non-selective transfer from primary school to secondary school, while opposed to the rapid and universal imposition of comprehensive secondary education everywhere.'[16] He pointed out that to have opposed all schemes would have involved repudiating some Conservative-controlled local authorities.

Thus comprehensive schools were accepted by the consensus. When Anthony Crosland issued the famous Circular 10/65 in the early days of the Labour Government he was passing on the experience of comprehensive schemes already gained by certain LEAs. Leicestershire, a Conservative education committee, was internationally known for its experiments launched in 1957. This and the LCC comprehensives – supported by reports from Sweden – provided ammunition. The mainstream in education accepted comprehensives more than either political party did: Sir Edward Boyle had to hold out against his reactionary elements but equally it took some effort in the Labour Party to shake off the allegiance to grammar schools. Local parent and teacher groups also started pushing for comprehensive schools.

When Labour came to power in 1964 there were 189 comprehensives in 39 authorities. By the time it was defeated in 1970 the number of comprehensives had risen to 1,300 schools educating 35 per cent of children (though some existed side-by-side with selective schools). This partnership of central government and local authorities discussed in chapter 2 had its effect upon the politics of the comprehensive school issue. It presented the Labour Government with a problem as to how they were to fulfil their commitment to comprehensive schools. They chose – bearing in mind their tiny majority in the House of Commons and the lack of money for new school building – not to argue that it was a matter of national direction but to rely on 'guidance', necessarily a kid-gloved process. Circular 10/65 did not tell local authorities to go comprehensive but requested them to submit plans for reorganizing on comprehensive lines, and this made it possible for local authorities to avoid the issue, to turn a deaf ear or to obstruct the process with plans which were not truly comprehensive. There was no doubt by the time Edward Short became Secretary of State for Education that the Government intended to have comprehensive schools, though the DES did little by way of proselytizing. Mr Short refused to give approval to new secondary building which was not comprehensive and introduced a bill attempting to make comprehensive reorganization compulsory upon local authorities, but before it could pass through the Commons his party had lost the general election.

When Edward Heath's Conservative Government came into office in 1970 there seemed to be a broad consensus in favour of comprehensive schools among the public and among local authorities. The majority of local authorities had submitted schemes to go comprehensive, and the movement seemed irrevocable. The principal issues had become the organization of comprehensive schools; how much, for example, did their success depend upon streaming or setting? were house systems useful? and, more controversially, should there be neighbourhood schools or schools with fixed proportions of different abilities? Resistance to comprehensives came from isolated pockets.

The new Secretary of State for Education and Science, Mrs Margaret Thatcher, set herself against the trend by issuing Circular 10/70 to revoke Circular 10/65. Like it, it was an unequivocally party political move, but it was also, as 10/65, rather less dogmatic than it might have been. It tended to reinforce existing administrative arrangements rather than make a new direction. It did not specifically object to comprehensives but withdrew the encouragement of central government for them, restating the autonomy of LEAs. Characteristically it was less this public statement than the use of administrative procedures which really restrained comprehensive development. Section 13 of the Education Act 1944 allows appeals to the Secretary of State against a local authority's intentions to change the nature of a school, and the Enfield case – one of the first victories of parent power, and anti-comprehensive – had ensured that reorganization of schools went through this process. Thus the Secretary of State was able to uphold objections to schemes and to save grammar schools. The arguments raised against comprehensive schemes usually involved two features: parents' freedom of choice of schools and the preservation of the best traditions of grammar schools.

The Secretary of State also used the Department of Education's controls over school building in the battle over comprehensives, just as Edward Short had done. Mrs Thatcher cut back all secondary school building in the first years of Conservative Government in the interests of directing the money available into the worthy cause of replacing old primary schools, and this had the effect of preventing LEAs from building comprehensive schools.

The actions of the Conservative Secretary of State made the reorganization of secondary education more contentious, and, in the sense of bashing opponents, more political. She erected the banner for those who disapproved of comprehensive schools on grounds of élitism, traditional values or freedom of choice. She polarized the situations in many localities. The arguments over reorganization became more intense than ever, and lobbies, petitions, vigils and various forms of protest action were used by opposing groups, by STEP (Stop the Eleven Plus) and by SOS (Save our Schools) and other groups. They were all characteristically local, though national bodies such as CASE, the Campaign for Comprehensive Education and the NEA provided an opportunity for co-ordination. The protests were often more specific than the plans for one local authority, concentrating on particular schools and the interests of its parents. Overall, despite the right-wing backlash, the progress towards a comprehensive system was inexorable, but individual authorities, or within them individual schools, continued to be selective. The educational arguments were not entirely settled. The High Master of Manchester Grammar School, Peter Mason, writing in *The Times* (14 July 1972) made it clear that the debate was by no means over. Defending direct grant schools, selection and parental choice, he pointed out 'that human beings are very differently endowed' and dismissed 'the doubtful satisfaction of theoretical egalitarianism'.

The local battle is repeated nationally only as Labour and Conservative Parties take up local issues and act out Government versus Opposition conflicts. The real debate is within the Conservative Party between centre elements, accepting comprehensive schools as part of a more egalitarian society, and traditionalists, arguing for a concept of individual freedom of choice which is perhaps consciously self-interested or perhaps a conviction about competitive society. And the Conservative Government claimed to be not opposed to comprehensives, only to particular implementations of the ideal. By October 1972 Mrs Thatcher had approved 2,300 proposals for comprehensives and rejected ninety-two. The readiness of that Government to uphold parents' objections and to accept arguments that loss of grammar schools infringed parents' opportunities of freedom of choice had a paradoxical effect on democracy in education. It listened to people – or some people – and boosted the parent movement, but it restricted equality of opportunity.

4 Positive discrimination

The contribution of comprehensive schools to equality of opportunity was in providing equal facilities and in not discriminating against working-class children by putting most of them in different and inferior schools. Comprehensive schools have delivered the goods in some senses: they have produced better examination passes and have proved that many children judged failures at the age of eleven have the ability to develop. What they have not delivered, however, is social equality. In fact, just as the comprehensive movement was getting underway, research was showing that there were more deep-rooted causes of inequality in education than comprehensive schools alone could hope to compensate for.

The shift of ground was in two directions. First, the environment and home background of pupils was seen as increasingly important as a determinant of educational performance. J. W. B. Douglas[17] showed significant variations in achievement among upper primary school children related to the social class of their families. Intelligence and ability were seen to depend on environment as well as innate factors. Second, attention was directed towards younger children. Jean Piaget and others pointed to the formative years and the effects of the first months and years of the child's life upon his subsequent achievement. In Britain the Plowden Report (1967)[18] pulled these various developments together. Commissioned to study primary schools, it examined the importance of home and family background, and of environment as well as heredity. Where forty years before Hadow had been told that intelligence grew at a standard rate and was related to certain innate characteristics, Plowden learnt of the interrelation of environment and heredity: 'Our argument . . . is that educational policy should explicitly recognise the power of the environment upon the school and of the school upon the environment.' The Plowden Report emphasized the relationship of a child's home and social background to his educational achievement. It found that the socio-economic group of parents related to their willingness to be involved in the affairs of the school and to encourage their children. It found that 29 per cent of households had five books or less. It saw, too, schools in deprived areas caught in vicious circles of hardship, unpleasant buildings, insufficient facilities, problem children. And it introduced to tackle this a new concept, 'positive discrimination', not equal facilities but extra facilities to compensate for other disadvantages. The main implementation of 'positive discrimination' was in the educational priority areas and in the Urban Aid Programmes. Both put additional resources into areas of need and concentrated particularly upon the nursery school, the playgroup and the pre-school child.

A. H. Halsey, national director of the action research teams on the educational priority areas, summed up the arguments for equality of opportunity which were overtaken by the concept of positive discrimination:[19]

> It may be said that liberal policies failed basically on an inadequate theory of learning. They failed to notice that the major determinants of educational attainment were not schoolmasters but social situations, not curriculum but motivation, not formal access to the school but support in the family and community.

He suggested what the new interpretation of equality of opportunity entailed:[20]

> A society affords equality of opportunity if the proportion of people from different social, economic or ethnic categories at all levels and in all types of education are more or less the same as the proportion of these people in the population at large.

In other words 'equality of opportunity' should not be 'equality of access' but 'equality of outcome'.

The problem has been tackled mostly at the pre-school level, working under the influence of research findings on the formative influence of this period of a child's development. It has thus coincided with a great concentration of interest in the pre-school child. Several of the pressure groups mentioned in chapter 4 were formed to attract attention to this area and to campaign for increased provision in a time of restraint. The Plowden-derived arguments about social deprivation combined with the increasingly articulate interests of women, the opportunities for women to work and to escape from the home in a way that seemed beneficial to their children, to campaign for the expansion of pre-school education. The direction of more resources into this area and the White Paper of December 1972[21] were universally welcomed by educational bodies and pressure groups. The only disagreement was whether enough was being provided. The consensus, established by the long build-up of pressure to remove the restrictions on the development of nursery education, achieved its aims partly at the expense of higher education, out of favour perhaps because of the image of students, perhaps because of the shock of finding that the nation has not been able to profitably employ all its graduates. *New Society* conducted a survey of its readers' opinions in 1972 (*New Society*, 7 December 1972) and found that 77 per cent of them agreed that education was our main hope for social change. Four times as many people thought there should be more pre-school education than supported higher education to create the kind of society and social values they sought.

Education is still regarded as the most likely means of creating a better society, but it is recognized that it has to enter into social factors in a way that 'secondary education for all' and 'grammar school education for all' never had to. The emphasis is on social as well as educational factors and an essential part of the Plowden and EPA thesis is that parents should be involved. The problem is which form of pre-school education is more likely to achieve the objectives, nursery schools with their professional standards and teacher-rather than parent-orientation or pre-school playgroups with mothers vitally involved but with less concern for standards. The White Paper's expansion of pre-school provision was an expansion of conventional ideas of schooling, in other words the outcome will be yet more school. It would, however, also be possible to take to heart the experience of playgroups and the demands for more participation – discussed in other chapters – so that education as schooling plays a subsidiary role. The search for equality of opportunity during this century has shown that the school system cannot come up with all the answers – but that it is all too likely to try.

References

1 Quoted in J. Stuart Maclure, *Educational Documents – England and Wales, 1816–1968*, Methuen, 1969, p. 173.
2 R. Barker, *Education and Politics 1900–1951*, Oxford University Press, London, 1972.
3 Quoted in ibid., p. 16.

4 Ibid., p. 18.
5 Hadow Report: *The Education of the Adolescent*, HMSO, London, 1927.
6 Ibid., p. xix.
7 Spens Report: *Secondary Education*, HMSO, London, 1939.
8 Norwood Report: *Curriculum and Examinations in Secondary Schools*, HMSO, London, 1943.
9 *Educational Reconstruction* (White Paper), HMSO, London, 1943: quoted in J. Stuart Maclure, op. cit., p. 206.
10 Spens Report, pp. 123–5.
11 Norwood Report, p. 3.
12 Spens Report, p. 71.
13 Quoted in C. Benn and B. Simon, *Half Way There*, McGraw-Hill, London, 1970, p. 21.
14 M. Parkinson, *The Labour Party and the Organization of Secondary Education 1918–65*, Routledge & Kegan Paul, London, 1970.
15 Quoted in ibid., p. 85.
16 *Leeds University Journal of Education, Administration and History*, Summer, 1972.
17 J. W. B. Douglas, *The Home and the School*, MacGibbon & Kee, London, 1964.
18 Plowden Report: *Children and their Primary Schools*, HMSO, London, 1967.
19 A. H. Halsey, *Educational Priority: EPA Problems and Policies*, vol. 1, HMSO, London, 1972, p. 8.
20 Ibid.
21 *Education: A Framework for Expansion* (White Paper), HMSO, London, 1972.

7 The challenge to traditional values

1 The politics of the curriculum

Arguments about the organization of schooling have been associated with political parties and with more generalized demands for social reform. Arguments about the content of education and about teaching methods have, on the whole, not been. They do, however, relate to one's concepts of society, now and in the future, and have a political basis and effect.

The processes of introducing changes into schools are, as we saw in chapter 5, uncertain; it is much easier to say whose responsibility it is not than whose it is. The major political parties have not normally regarded it as their responsibility: the conventional attitude is that the most they can do is to provide the framework and facilities in which teachers can give of their best. The Secretary of State for Education and Science disclaims all responsibility for the curriculum, quite properly turning aside all embarrassing questions about political bias, the immorality of sex education or the efficiency of Latin grammar classes. The Secretary of State does perhaps through his speeches and less public comments take part in forming public opinion or in, variously, reflecting the real nature of people's attitudes, speaking up for ordinary folk or the silent majority. This sounds a phoney business but, given the system of nudges and hints through which the education system works, the Secretary of State has an impact.

The DES has a more permanent and far-reaching impact through its administrative guidance and controls, though, as we saw in chapter 1, it would disclaim any political involvement. It is also not directly involved in curriculum matters, though it feels a responsibility for good practice in the schools and for the development of the service. These concepts assume a continual move by the consensus to more progressive ideas. In this, therefore, and in considering the reasons for and effects of administrative measures the DES is bound to have attitudes about curriculum matters – or, perhaps one should say, have attitudes about other people's opinions on curriculum matters. The HMIs, who are attached to the DES, are concerned with what happens in schools in terms of efficiency and co-ordinate development around the country. They may also help disseminate ideas for new methods and changes in content proposed by the Schools Council and other bodies. The HMIs are engaged in processes of consultation and persuasion, of bringing people and ideas together, rather than making any policies or exercising controls. Local education authorities with their formal responsibilities for schools act similarly, reserving curriculum and teaching methods to schools, their headteachers and staffs. Both the dissemination and implementation of ideas depends upon general agreement; the processes of change and innovation are mysterious.

In the classroom, therefore, the introduction of new methods is very much left to the teacher and his headteacher, and becomes a matter of individual preferences and politics. There is no national or local policy and the teacher is not supported in any attempts to be more progressive, to get one step ahead. The unions are not involved beyond their membership of the Schools Council and occasional consultation and presentation of evidence. Thus the response of education and curricula to social change is difficult to establish and certainly has no direct decision-making relationship. There is, however, a total effect, a combination of institutions and people having made up their minds and having acted together, and this effect is political. For individuals and for the system there are politics which can be identified, for example, in class bias, conflict between conservatives and progressives, and in terminology.

Changes in society, either actual or potential, do not produce radical curricula. One has only to think about the problems which have caught public attention very recently – of women, immigrants and minorities – to see that in the main they are not helped by school, no more than are most curricula really adapted to future society. There is, none the less, a backlash against modern methods parallel to that against the alleged permissiveness of television and the arts and the breakdown of standards in society as a whole. There are demands for a return to the old certainties of academic standards in schools. Dr Harry Judge, much respected headmaster of Banbury School, one of the largest comprehensive schools, told the North of England Education Conference in January 1973 that the time had come for headteachers 'to reassert the priority of intellectual and academic aims within schools' and to redress the balance away from social objectives. And on the right the Black Papers blamed progressive methods for a decline in standards.

An area in which this kind of politics is evident is that of literacy. The values of society have changed in such a way that schools concentrating upon traditional concepts of literacy seem to be facing an increasingly uphill struggle. Traditional culture in the arts has been undermined by more popular movements: intellectuals have become prepared to accept pop as valid art, and the exclusiveness and minority-interest of traditional arts have been held against them. The relevance of traditional standards of culture to modern society are also in doubt. More specifically in the area of literacy, Marshall McLuhan has welcomed a world in which electronic communications are more important than the printed word, thus devaluing reading as a skill. In our everyday experience, children are entertained by watching television rather than reading books.

At the same time it has become clear that the traditional values of literacy were far from universal even within our society, and that they were closer to middle-class than working-class values. With present concepts of social justice it has not been possible to conclude, as formerly one could, that therefore the working classes should be educated to the same standards. There may have been a reverse movement in which, as in the arts, working-class – and majority – values have been taken on board by the middle classes.

Something similar has happened in schools. The work of Basil Bernstein on children's language has produced a theory of two different codes of language used by different social classes, an elaborated code associated with the middle class and a restricted code associated with the unskilled working class. The elaborated code is more appropriate to concept formation, to abstract thought and reasoning, whereas the restricted code is closer to immediate experiences. Schools rely on elaborated codes, and are therefore both more comfortable to and more sympathetic with middle-class children. The theory has created a dilemma. On one hand, it is characteristic of the education service that the theory in practice usually provides another excuse for why working-class children do not prosper. But, on the other hand, as Bernstein argues, the more democratic conclusion is that schools should adapt themselves to this different use of language with all its different implications for the kinds of learning it encourages. Thus schools are faced with a political choice on language: if they maintain their present attitudes they are acting against the working class.

However, the argument is not seen simply in social terms. There may be different attitudes towards literacy but they have not taken root so strongly that people are prepared to accept that standards of literacy – in the sense of a grading in the ability to read – should change. If society does not need or does not think traditional literacy is appropriate, it would be reasonable to argue against worrying if schools no longer supply it. There is evidence that reading standards have not risen in recent years, and fears that they have fallen. The NFER report on *The Trend in Reading Standards* in 1972 found that reading standards among eleven-year-olds were the same as in 1960 and that a slight improvement detected in 1964 had been lost. This, together with other more scary reports, prompted a good deal of public concern and the establishment of the Bullock Committee to investigate. Supporters of traditional methods were quick to blame the 'new-fangled' ways of teaching reading and prompted a fairly general agreement that some progressive methods had lacked structure and rigour.

A report of the Inner London Education Authority in December 1972 summed up some of the problems:[1]

There is a further complex problem which derives from the ambivalent attitude of both the teacher and the world outside school. Understanding of the way in which language develops and of its role in the learning process and in individual development has led English teachers to put greater emphasis on talk in the classroom, between individuals and within groups. At the same time the development of audio and visual media has led to the use of means other than the written language as stimulus to talk or for providing subject matter for talk. Outside the school, the exploitation of new media has tended to reduce dependence on the written word for necessary communication, information and entertainment. In many occupations, and not only the unskilled and manual, the work of the day can be conducted without reference to the printed word in any form. Acceptance of the primacy of the spoken word both in teaching and in affairs outside the school has weakened motivation for learning to read and write. Because life can be lived and indeed is lived adequately without such skills and since for many their acquisition presents such difficulty, one increasingly hears arguments for regarding them as of reduced significance.

Traditionalists exploited concern over reading standards, blaming less authoritarian methods of teaching and the emphasis on creative writing over correct grammar, and linking it to the shift from traditional culture. Professor Brian Cox, Professor of English at Manchester University, at the conference of the National Council for Educational Standards in January 1973 spoke of 'a crisis of verbal culture' in which children being deprived of the traditional heritage of their culture were the 'new deprived of the twentieth century'. The 'Arnoldian concept' that there was a tradition of high culture which it was the responsibility of an élite to keep up was, he said, being displaced by ideas based on fashionable sociology. Standards of clarity and worth were under attack from relativist thinking, an emphasis on the anti-rational and a search for a culture not imposed from above. These neo-progressive views thought that working-class speech had a vitality which was as valid as correct English, and this was 'absurd'. There was, he said, a need to make changes, however, but so as to achieve traditional objects more efficiently.

Thus what might be termed purely educational concerns, such as the ability of children to read, become intertwined with arguments about social and cultural values and with arguments about tradition and progress. But this debate is avoided by educational bodies, politicians, administrators or unions, except in terms of their conception of purely educational standards. One has to turn to newspaper correspondence columns for selections of letters which deplore changing social standards and correlate them with lack of discipline and an alleged reduction in educational standards. Whatever pretence is made that politics can be kept out of education, when parents and public are drawn to comment they talk about good manners, discipline as a value in itself, correct behaviour and order, or else about the lack of relevance of schools to society. An editorial in the *Spectator* (6 January 1973) illustrated such a concern for loss of values, bringing in the problem of immigration for good measure:

There is increasingly clear evidence that the number of illiterates – and even of innumerates – in the country is on the increase; and that there is an increasing proportion of people under twenty-five among those of our citizens who cannot read. Worse, as the evidence presented by the Community Relations Commission to the Bullock inquiry into literacy in Britain demonstrates, increasing numbers of immigrant children and increasing numbers of coloured children born in this country, find it more and more difficult to break through the language barrier of their new home, largely because teaching standards in English are so low, and because the theories of education currently fashionable in our schools encourages the indulgence of childish personality at the expense of linguistic and cultural training. If serious racial conflict is to break out in Britain before the end of the century, liberal educationalists will be among those most responsible, because they have, designedly and deliberately, refused to provide coloured British and immigrant youth with the tools of survival in our community, most notable among which is a sound command, on traditional and grammatical lines, of the language. A majority of modern educational theorists, and a great number of modern teachers, prefer to indulge their own psychological fantasies – arrayed in the tawdry guise of a concern for the emotional freedom of children under their care – at the expense of those skills they are employed by the taxpayer and expected by most parents to teach. Thus our offspring leave their schools increasingly incompetent, in morals, in discipline, in cultivation, in responsibility, and, above all, in literacy.

A couple of weeks later one could have found in a local paper, the *Newham Recorder* (18 January 1973), an interview with a local teacher retiring in distress at the loss of standards, at the illiteracy of school leavers, associating it with rudeness among pupils, long hair among some young teachers and vandalism: 'The failure in education must pose a threat to the future of the nation as a whole. I feel very gloomy about the future. So many aspects of life today seem to involve cocking a snook at authority.'

There are plenty of examples, and one does not have to reach far to make links with accusations of propaganda in teaching about South Africa or left-wing bias in a hymn book striving for relevance to the lives of the pupils. Or, of course, to sex education. But if we look at other issues in educational reform we can examine further the relationship between education and changing social objectives.

2 Not so much a classroom . . .

Attempts to expand equality of opportunity at secondary level, as discussed in the last chapter, were tackled mostly in terms of the organization of schooling, but comprehensive schools have raised doubts about the appropriateness of traditional grammar school curricula for all pupils, developing to a more sophisticated level the theme of the Hadow Report that different children have different aptitudes. The greatest changes in curriculum and teaching methods have been in primary schools, the British primary school becoming a source of national pride in the 1960s. Although it isn't possible to define exactly how or why the new methods were introduced, they can be associated with certain changes in society and changes in the social objectives of education.

New teaching methods are a challenge to traditional ideas both of learning and authority. The traditional concept is that subjects are bodies of knowledge to be taught and this relates to a particular concept of authority. If one believes, for example, that geography consists of a defined set of knowledge taught by experts, then one teaches it as an expert, demanding that children sit quiet, listen and take notes, memorizing the facts. But if one sees learning not as subject-based but child-based, one thinks not of facts to be learnt but of skills to be acquired, then this requires less formal, less authoritarian forms of organization so that the child can experiment for himself. Project-based methods in primary and secondary schools, such as Nuffield science and maths, begin in the child's immediate experience and then encourage him to reach out for what he needs to learn through a number of subjects and methods of learning. Textbooks become just another source of knowledge rather than the be-all and end-all of teaching.

Headteacher John Mitchell writes in *Education for Democracy* of the adults' response on visiting a new primary school:[2]

> They remember the authoritarian approach of their childhood
> and are puzzled when they discover that their children are not
> taught in the same way. . . . To the uninformed a walk round
> the modern primary school can be a confusing experience.
> No longer are the children rigidly marshalled in long silent

lines. Nor will a glance through a classroom window reveal neat rows of desks occupied by silent listening children. . . . The first impression will be that this building exists to be used by children.

The new methods are by no means universal. The Plowden Report in 1967 found that about a third of schools had been substantially affected by the new approaches, a third somewhat affected and a third very little. In primary schools learning by discovery methods have broken down the idea of subject and authoritarian hierarchies; children have to be free to follow their own learning. Individual children in a classroom will be reading, painting, playing. John Mitchell explains:[3]

> The modern primary school aims to awaken the child's interest in learning, to view each child as an individual and cater for him accordingly, to give each child the opportunity to produce creative work and to experience the satisfaction which accompanies the achievement of original and valuable work. The school in no way aims to compare one child with another, but only to compare what each child is now producing with what he has previously produced.

The school aims to foster 'self-confidence, initiative, responsibility, respect and understanding for others' as well as intellectual development.

Why should these new ideas have developed in the primary schools? They are not all new in themselves; it is not that new research has been rushed into classroom practice; most of the ideas have been in circulation since the late nineteenth century. No conclusive statements can be made of why the thing should have gelled in the past thirty years, but there is a mixture of factors, of educational theory and of social, political and economic circumstances. Some of these are hard to define beyond the recognition that our society and its ideas of authority have changed.

In the DES's booklet, *Inside the Primary School*, John Blackie attempts to trace the processes of innovation and looks back to the late 1930s:[4]

> Firstly, however gingerly some teachers grasped it, the freedom of the individual headteacher was genuine. He had a far wider latitude in deciding what to teach, how to teach it and what

books to use than was or is enjoyed by the headteachers in any other country in the world. Secondly, the influences at work on him were becoming more experimental in outlook. The training colleges rather slowly, H.M. Inspectorate more quickly, became the agents of innovation. In-service training courses . . . began to increase. The Hadow report on *The Primary School* (1931) was beginning to be read and it gave respectability to ideas which had hitherto been thought cranky or idealistic.

Professor G. W. Bassett of Queensland University, in a study of English and American primary education, explains the import of research and theory:[5]

English education on the whole has been pragmatic, and not explicitly based on theorizing of any sort. The main role that theory appears to have played is to support procedures sanctioned by usage and 'common sense'. In the first third of this century Froebelian influence was perhaps the strongest, and was exploited effectively by those concerned with the education of young children. The education of infants through free discipline and play has been a feature of English education for the past thirty years. Those concerned with older children, on the other hand, for whom it was believed more didactic teaching was necessary, have not had the same kind of support. More recently, however, the writings of Piaget have been influencing English education strongly. The theory of a progression in cognitive development through levels with qualitative differences accords well with the 'common-sense' notions that teachers have about children's mental development from concrete to abstract forms. . . . And it stresses the importance of the interaction of the learner with his environment. . . .

Headteacher Arthur Razzell in *Education for Democracy*[6] adds social changes and the need to cater for the 'explosion of knowledge' and notes:

It is not sound economics to prepare the nation's children for a way of life which has already ceased to exist. In Edwardian days there was a need for an adequate supply of counting-house clerks and literate workmen. Today there is a need for men and women with more sophisticated skills.

Maybe we are also more concerned to be kind to little children and to allow fun. Attitudes may have been affected by the evidence of ethologists on the value of play as learning, and there have been developed for grown-ups also more sophisticated games and techniques of learning by simulation. We have also come to trust the home, at least the middle-class home, rather more, and schools have adjusted to the pressure for parents, particularly mothers, to be involved in their children's education. A further social change is sometimes suggested, that mothers and women teachers have taken over primary education from men, and that partly because of this maternal values have been given greater currency.

Primary schools are also, as elementary schools in the 1920s and 1930s were not for all children, a first stage in education. Children then go on to secondary schools where, it may be thought, the real learning and training for examinations begins. In some secondary schools there are also many changes – integrated studies, project work, a more relaxed atmosphere, fewer rules and regulations. The bases of new methods in primary schools are not, however, the same as those of most secondary school teaching which is still more traditional and subject-based. Children from primary schools may appear in secondary schools to have learnt less than they used to when actually they have learnt differently. This misconception may be behind accusations that new-fangled methods have caused a decline in standards. But there is still an attitude in secondary schools that children should be knocked into shape. A teacher dismissed from a comprehensive school, Mrs Lonca Rousseau, told *Time Out* (30 July–5 August 1971) of her head of department having said, 'You've got to break that Stephen. He's too cocky, I can see him as a shop steward. We've got to break him' – a sharp contrast in political as well as human attitudes to the desire to foster 'self-confidence, initiative, responsibility, respect and understanding for others'.

3 Competition

Secondary education has been founded on the idea of children competing against each other, on education as a process of selection. In the original ideal the exams and the tests at 11-plus were to identify different aptitudes among children, but in practice the selection was by competitive exam for places in grammar schools. Children were then streamed according to their IQ and/or their success in termly and yearly exams. It has been possible to identify streams making for GCE and university entry, for O-level, and for early leaving. Secondary schools have predominantly stuck to the traditional values of exam passing and more traditional concepts of knowledge.

The Plowden Report found that in primary schools streaming was losing favour and welcomed this trend. Its arguments against streaming were, it said, the same as those against 11-plus selection: 'The accuracy of the selective process, the contrast in the provision made for children of differing ability and the effect of segregating them on their achievement.' There was also evidence that streaming was 'a means of social selection' in that a higher proportion of middle-class children were in upper streams than their test scores warranted.

Research has not established a case either for or against streaming in terms of efficiency in teaching. It is clear, however, that, as J. W. B. Douglas writes, 'streaming by ability reinforces the process of social selection': 'Children who come from well-kept homes and who are themselves clean, well-clothed and shod, stand a greater chance of being put in the upper streams than their measured ability would seem to justify.'[7]

In other words, attempts to extend equality of opportunity are being hindered by teachers' prejudices. Furthermore: 'Once there they are likely to stay and to improve in performance in succeeding years. This is in striking contrast to the deterioration noticed in those children of similar initial measured ability who were placed in lower streams.'[8] Not only is streaming unfair, it also tends to increase inequalities.

The idea of streaming is based on the idea of fixed intelligence, as in the Hadow Report which established the tripartite system of secondary schools. Now, however, intelligence is recognized as a much more variable and fluid thing, and it is seen that as children are given a wider range of subjects so different children can shine in them. Thus the evaluation of academic ability as the top stream combined with its social class bias make streaming a means of encouraging only certain kinds of children. Mixed ability groups and setting by which children are streamed differently in different subjects have proved to be as efficient educationally and more just socially.

Streaming is, perhaps because of its class bias, an emotive subject. As Professor G. W. Bassett noted the NFER research showed that teachers in streamed schools were older, used more formal methods, were less permissive, had a lower tolerance to noise and favoured the A stream: 'The supporters of streaming are expressing a whole cluster of attitudes about education concerning the curriculum, discipline, academic achievement, and so on; and, just as obviously the opponents of streaming oppose the things that go with it.'[9]

Like streaming, attitudes to examinations relate to teachers' political attitudes and to the social objectives of education. The object of school for the most 'educated' section of the population is the passing of an examination and a certificate proving it. This certificate can then be reported to employers and friends in an effort to win jobs and esteem; society grades people by their achievement in exams. Common sense and research confirm that exam results are not necessarily a guide to any ability other than the ability to pass exams, and the search for more meaningful tests has led to new forms of examination and assessment.

In schools the most radical move has been the introduction of the Certificate of Secondary Education, an exam which was devised so that pupils of average ability in any subject would be able to gain a certificate. The introduction of CSE was radical not only in this extension of opportunity but in that it broke away from having exams and syllabuses set by an outside authority. It recognized that if teachers wanted a form of assessment for their pupils it was right that they should have control or influence in what was assessed. There are three forms of the exam, known as modes: Mode 1 is a conventional externally set and marked exam; Mode 3 allows teachers to set their own syllabuses and to mark the exams, moderated by external assessors; Mode 2 is a compromise between the other two. Thus CSE represents part of the movement away from respect for authority and towards teacher participation, although it is also a recognition of the teachers' control over teaching methods and content. New exams common to all at sixteen will be more like CSE than GCE and an A-level CSE – the Certificate of Extended Education – will provide an assessment of the 'new sixth formers', the less academic who stay on into the sixth forms in increasing numbers.

The search for new forms of assessment in the sixth form – for exams that are a better prediction of university success and/or more useful to the less academic sixth former – and the move towards CSE-type exams has met strong opposition from traditionalists. Professor Arthur Pollard, a Black Paper contributor, told the conference of the National Council for Educational Standards in January 1973:[10]

> Make no mistake – the crucial battle for those of us who care about standards will be fought in the coming months in the field of examinations. . . . The conflict is clear – on the one hand, teacher-controlled, locally determined, possibly continuously assessed no-fail examinations with all their diversity of content and standard, or externally conducted examinations which, whilst allowing some degree of choice and emphasis, are controlled and standardized both in syllabus and marking and are possessed of an impartiality that no CSE-type examination can possibly attain. . . . By its fragmentation the CSE method represents movement away from cultural unity to diversity, to the deliberate breakdown of such unity of values and knowledge that our society still possesses. . . . The breakdown of values may indeed be the subtle aim of some of the proponents of the new methods.

From his side of the fence there is scorn of those who try to assert equality by doing away with exams and with the use of exams to grade people. Professor Pollard in this same speech mocked the idea by quoting Gilbert and Sullivan:

> Lord Chancellors were cheap as sprats,
> And Bishops in their shovel hats
> Were plentiful as tabby cats –
> In point of fact, too many.

Approval of examinations is linked with approval of an élite and of traditional, fixed standards against which people can be tested. There is sometimes an implication that competition is the life-blood of society and that to do away with selection is to turn education into a cloud-cuckoo land. Could anything be more ridiculous than the idea that people should not be failed, says the argument; is not life a rat-race?

The defence of examinations is increasingly a retreat. Even a

Secretary of State, Mr Edward Short, referred to them as a mill-stone round secondary schools' necks. CASE in its evidence for a new Education Act stated:[11]

> We would like to see a less competitive and selective pattern
> of education. We believe that the influence of streaming,
> selection, and competitive examinations on the life and work
> of a school has many educational and social disadvantages.

The Schools Council in its deliberations about sixth-form exams proposed a system of grading for A-levels in which there would be no pass-fail, instead a twenty-point grading. It was rejected by the Conservative Secretary of State, Mrs Thatcher, who said she had been unable to find a consensus in its favour, noting that it was important not to 'reduce the confidence in the examinations or to reduce their acceptability by the public at large'.

As the Secretary of State implied, exams are seen by many people as the proof of education and for parents it may seem essential that their children can take examination passes into the outside world. It has also been suggested that it is through examinations that schools are accountable to the public and by which the performance of the school and teachers, as much as that of the pupils, can be assessed.

It is also true, however, that nearly half the pupils who leave school do so not only without any passes but also without there having been any examination appropriate to their ability, and that in this there is a very strong bias in social class. It has increasingly been made apparent that the experience of failure has a bad effect on people and that streaming and exams in themselves are self-fulfilling prophecies.

In *Education for Democracy* Arthur Rowe attacks the traditional-ists:[12]

> The fear of the traditionalists is that this (competitive and
> acquisitive) ethic and its underlying assumptions will be
> abandoned: only by keeping it can they be sure of hanging on
> to their present class monopoly of quality education. . . .
> They defend their brutalizing and stigmatizing strategies,
> which reject the majority and give a sense of inferiority, of
> failure or partial failure, by claiming that they are necessary
> for the sake of that highly intelligent minority upon which

the country depends, as it has always depended. But the only kind of intelligence they recognize is the one they narcissistically believe they've got a monopoly of.

One has, he says, to take 'an optimistic, democratic view of all pupils, their nature and potentiality':[13]

Schools which adopt an ethic of co-operation and community can create a milieu which is quickly accepted as natural and which will in time change class-biased assumptions into humane and democratic ones, accepted implicitly and unconsciously. A milieu in which all their pupils will grow, not only in brotherly awareness of one another as of equal worth, but also in generous and sensitive recognition of each other's valuable and infinitely varied qualities and gifts.

References

1 *Evidence by the Inner London Education Authority to the Committee of Enquiry into the Teaching of Reading and the Use of the English Language*, 1972, p. 6.
2 D. Rubinstein and C. Stoneman (eds), *Education for Democracy*, Penguin, Harmondsworth, 1972, 2nd edn, pp. 98–9.
3 Ibid., p. 100.
4 J. Blackie, *Inside the Primary School*, HMSO, London, 1967, p. 9.
5 G. W. Bassett, *Innovation in Primary Education*, Wiley, London, 1970, pp. 42–4.
6 Rubinstein and Stoneman, op. cit., p. 119.
7 J. W. B. Douglas, *The Home and the School*, MacGibbon & Kee, London, 1964, and Panther, London, 1967, p. 150.
8 Ibid.
9 Bassett, op. cit., p. 47.
10 Quoted in *The Accountability of Schools*, Churchill Press, Enfield, 1973, pp. 28–48.
11 *Parents and the Major New Education Act*, CASE, 1969.
12 Rubinstein and Stoneman, op. cit., p. 21–2.
13 Ibid., p. 25.

8 The expansion of education

1 More school

Public authorities in England and Wales spent £2,268 million on education in 1970–1, topping the magic £2,000 million for the first time. Schools spent £1,255 million and universities £253 million. Together the service had been growing at a rate of 10·8 per cent a year for a decade. Looking back over seventy years, expenditure by local education authorities had increased by 110 times.[1]

When the Robbins Committee[2] investigated the expansion of the universities it pointed out that in 1900 25,000 students were in full-time higher education; in 1962 there were 216,000. The White Paper, *Education: A Framework for Expansion*,[3] envisaged that in Great Britain in 1981 there would be 750,000 places in higher education institutions. This would cater for 22 per cent of the age-group compared to 7 per cent in 1961 and 15 per cent in 1971. In England and Wales in 1960 one-third of boys and girls stayed on beyond the leaving age of fifteen, in 1971 56·3 per cent; in 1955 4·5 per cent of their age-group passed two or more GCE A-levels, in 1971 12 per cent.[4]

There are endless statistics which produce equally awesome impressions of the size of the expansion of education both in terms of expenditure and numbers in schools and universities, justified on account of the benefits to individuals and to society. A common theme, as discussed in chapter 6, has been the attempt to increase equality of opportunity. The expansion in numbers has been in part voluntary but the overwhelming change this century has been a massive spread of compulsory full-time education provided free for a progressively greater number of years. School attendance was made compulsory initially to prevent the exploitation of child labour but the service developed and decided that all should share in its benefits.

The concept of free compulsory school is now fundamental to the whole system and those who work in it. A continuing problem is its relationship with independent, fee-paying schools. Independent schools have been attacked from the left-wing as the bastions of privilege, and the public schools are the obsession of sections of the Labour Party as we saw in chapter 1. An eccentric and experimental fringe of schools like Summerhill has been tolerated but the dominant progressive tone has been of disapproval.

School and university education has consistently been seen as a means to provide more education and from a progressive point of view to rectify social injustices. Schools have been made free and compulsory to achieve these objectives. But amongst the natural tendencies to proceed on with the future and accept projections based on these institutions there are alternatives suggested, some of which challenge these concepts.

2 Raising the leaving age

The number of years which children have attended school has increased steadily, both voluntarily and compulsorily. From progressive quarters there has generally been a demand for the compulsory raising of the school leaving age as a means of spreading the benefits of education. The problem has always been that the children who stay at school voluntarily and then proceed to college or university tend to be the children of more fortunate families living in more fortunate areas. The children who leave at the minimum statutory age are usually described as the less intelligent and the under-achievers from culturally deprived homes. In 1971 44 per cent of boys and girls left school at the minimum age, and 77 per cent had left by the age of sixteen.

A clear statement of the relationship between social class and school achievement was provided by the research of J. W. B. Douglas, J. M. Ross and H. R. Simpson into 5,000 children born in the first week of March 1946. Reporting on the progress of these children to the age of sixteen-plus, the researchers concluded in *All Our Future*:[5]

> The social class pattern of leaving may be summarized by saying that the upper middle class pupils were two and a half times as likely to stay on after the minimum leaving age as the

lower manual working class pupils, four times as likely to complete the session 1961/2 [i.e. the end of the fifth form] and nearly six times as likely to start the session 1962/3 [i.e. entering in most cases the sixth form].

They calculated that because of early leaving and low aspirations probably 5 per cent of the next generation of manual workers would be recruited from pupils who with better social circumstances might have qualified for administrative or professional qualifications. They found that, for example, upper middle-class children of high ability completed GCE O-level stage and stayed into the sixth year in 90 per cent of cases, lower middle-class 78 per cent, upper manual working-class 67 per cent, lower manual working-class 50 per cent.

And the same relationships were evident with children of low ability where children of the upper middle class stayed on in 20 per cent of cases, lower middle class 8 per cent, upper manual working class 3 per cent, lower manual working class 2 per cent. And the same relationships were evident in good examination passes where upper middle-class children were successful in 77 per cent of cases, lower middle-class in 60 per cent, upper manual working-class in 53 per cent, lower manual working-class in 37 per cent.

The figures point out forcefully both the lack of opportunity some children have to make good and the lack of benefit some children draw from the education system in terms of the years they use it. It has seemed necessary to compel less fortunate children to stay on at school. It has been argued that the State has a duty to ensure some equality of provision in this respect and has been argued that voluntary staying on did not allow free choice for children from deprived areas because the norms of their culture and family would almost force them to leave school. It was therefore the duty of the State to make staying on compulsory.

In the Education Act 1918 the leaving age was set at fourteen. The Labour Party's policies of 'secondary education for all' and the Hadow Report (1926) demanded that it be raised to fifteen, but economic circumstances and Conservative Governments defeated them. A compulsory minimum leaving age of fifteen was not achieved until after the Education Act 1944. Even then the first act of the new minister of education, Mr R. A. (later Lord) Butler, was to postpone the date until 1947. The education service remained dedicated to the raising of the leaving age to sixteen, and this was achieved in 1972–3.

The Crowther Report, *15 to 18* (1959), one of the series of major reports from the Central Advisory Council, summarized the current concern in two main arguments:[6]

> One starts from the social and personal needs of 15 year-olds, and regards education as one of the basic rights of the citizen; ... Nothing has happened in the last twenty years, or could happen, which would weaken our agreement with the view of John Dewey that what the best and wisest parent wants for his own child the community must want for all its children. A boy or girl of 15 is not sufficiently mature to be exposed to the pressures of the world of industry or commerce. ... Until they are 16, boys and girls need an environment designed for their needs. Each extension of the school leaving age obviously brings the schools increasingly difficult emotional and social problems, especially perhaps with the education of girls. But the difficulty of the problems is no reason for refusing to face them. ...
> We may hide, but we do not solve, teenage problems simply by letting boys and girls leave school.

The second argument was headed 'National Considerations', concerned 'with education as a vital part of the nation's capital investment':[7]

> It is unlikely that, without compulsion, it will become the accepted thing in all classes of society for boys and girls of average intelligence to stay at school until 16. ... We believe the odds are weighted against the national interest.

The average worker needed much more education than in the past, partly because of the roads opened upwards for the more intelligent and partly because of increase in numbers of skilled and professional posts; what Crowther called a 'universal upgrading'.

In January 1968 the Labour Government committed one of its notable reversals of policy by postponing the raising of the leaving age until 1972–3 because of the economic situation. Its action evoked strong protests from educational groups and unions, with the exception of the NAS who believed that the schools were unprepared for the new older pupils. The General Secretary of the NUT, Sir Ronald Gould, argued: 'Only an extended school life will enable the country to tap the full potential of ability available and develop the skills on which our economic recovery will largely depend' (*Education*, 12 January 1968).

The Labour Party may yet propose a further raising of the leaving age to rectify continuing disparities. It may prefer to encourage young people to enter further education, however, and this may reduce the demand for more compulsory schooling. The Conservative Secretary of State, Mrs Margaret Thatcher, appears, as Conservative Governments have in the past, to think that the process has gone far enough, and the general tendency is to prefer now to channel resources to increase equality of opportunity into, for example, pre-school education.

But whilst it has been conventionally accepted as progressive to make people stay at school longer, certain factors have conflicted with this. There has been the trend towards earlier maturity among young people. Legally, the age of majority was reduced from twenty-one to eighteen by recommendation of the Latey Commission in 1967. Biologically people grow up faster and bigger. Culturally teenage values have been accepted and economically young people have been able to be more independent.

It is also obvious that many children do not want to stay at school. The general thesis has been that parents were responsible either, in middle-class families, for encouraging children to stay or, in working-class families, to leave, in both cases regardless of their ability or potential. Some research supports, however, the reports of teachers that the children themselves are only too eager to leave, to leave the restrictive childlike environment of school and enter the real, wage-earning world. A survey of 2,000 thirteen-year-olds in Oxford by Donald Hutchings and Judy Bradley (*New Society*, 31 August 1972) showed that one in four wanted to leave school as soon as they could, although two-thirds of them said their parents would like them to continue. The authors pointed out:

> Not only are these 15 year olds thoroughly frustrated by the school situation, but they also lack the basic skills for success with most forms of school work. In our discussions with them, their chief complaints were that they were 'treated like kids', that they were always being 'bossed about', and that they could not wear what they wanted. They felt that most school subjects were a 'waste of time'.

There is also opposition among teachers, which, if expressed publicly, is usually counted as reactionary or simply pessimistic. The leaderships and policies of the main teaching unions, with qualifications from the NAS, are for the raising of the leaving age. The NAS, which is taken to be the more right wing of the teacher unions, has in recent years opposed and marginally accepted the raising of the leaving age. At its annual conference in April 1972 President Ray Holden put the arguments against (*Education*, April 1972, p. 328):

> Few would oppose the extension of compulsory schooling in an ideal society, but our society is far from ideal; the preparations are still incomplete, curriculum development projects in many areas are scarcely off the ground, the promised building programme is only partially carried out. Worst of all is the evidence of reluctance and lack of co-operation from the pupils themselves. Nearly 55 per cent stayed on voluntarily in 1970, compared with 43 per cent in 1967 and 26 per cent in 1955. It would not have taken very long to have achieved 75 per cent and the rest need not be deprived of all opportunities to obtain full-time education.

He proposed an alternative: 'Could they not be credited with one year's full time education to be taken at any time in an institution of the student's own choice, providing he or she could convince the establishment of his suitability for that course?'

The extent of opposition among teachers has been larger than union leaderships and policies have acknowledged. Their opposition is based partly on a fear that insufficient resources have been supplied to do the job properly, partly a belief that resources could be better directed elsewhere but also a recognition that the pupils are too big and too resentful to be treated as children – and perhaps a certain physical fear. The Wolverhampton association of the NAS found in a small survey of its members (*New Schoolmaster*, June 1972) that 67 per cent of them were opposed to the raising of the leaving age in principle and 88 per cent to doing it in 1973.

Is opposition to the raising of the leaving age an expression of the backwardness of some teachers and of the inability of some teenagers to recognize their real interests? The leaving age has now been raised but none the less the debate continues. To be committed to it implies a conviction that school is a 'good thing' in itself and that the unfairness of the middle class's greater use and benefits from school are best solved by forcing everyone to have more. One might argue, as the Crowther Report did, on the basis of national or individual benefit. It does, however, seem less obvious now than it did to Crowther in 1959 that school is 'an environment designed for [fifteen-year-olds'] needs'. Although the main trend of arguments has divided between, on the left, demands for greater equality and for this social good to be promoted through compulsion and, on the right, for *laissez-faire* and self-interest, there is now evidence and radical arguments about alternatives which question not the need to encourage equality but the value of school as a means to it. These arguments may seem to have more in common with what have been considered anti-progressive views in that they object in some way to school.

3 Further education

One alternative form of public education in the United Kingdom which is too frequently neglected in debate and planning is that provided by the further education system, which offers a different institutional framework for those of post-school age and which could be applied to fifteen-year-olds in their final year of school. Technical and further education colleges offer a wide variety of courses in technical, vocational and more academic subjects, GCE as well as craft and trade qualifications. Its courses may be taken full-time, part-time, in evening classes or as sandwich courses with periods in industry.

In recent years there has been a spontaneous movement, un-measured but of considerable significance, from school sixth forms to further education colleges. Students who would have stayed in the school sixth form to take A-levels as well as the so-called 'new sixth formers' (the academically less able who want to continue their education but may not pass A-levels) have gone to technical colleges. There they have apparently found an environment more suited to their needs, more independent, non-custodial, with a wide choice of subjects to study, many of them more relevant to a future career. In a few local authorities this movement threatened to take on such proportions that technical colleges have been banned from offering A-levels and the students forced back into schools or out to work. More generally, however, it has been accepted, and a number of LEAS are working towards amalgamating sixth forms and FE colleges. Sixth-form colleges may not include craft and vocational subjects, but others, perhaps 'sixth-form colleges', 'tertiary colleges' or just 'colleges' may bring together academic and vocational, sharing staff and facilities and offering a wide selection of courses. The logistics of comprehensive schools which cannot individually support a viable sixth form have encouraged the amalgamation of sixth forms into such colleges as well as recognition of students' preferences. There have been proposals that the regulations concerning school sixth forms and FE colleges for the sixteen to nineteen age-range should be standardized or that all should be worked into a 'tertiary' stage of education. Schools Council working parties have studied the question of sixteen to nineteen education and appropriate exams.

Students at school for the extra year could make use of further education facilities, though the DES has made sure that they are based in school even if they go to techs for a day or two a week. A compromise solution is 'linked courses'. But there is a widespread fear among schoolteachers that technical colleges lack the pastoral care of schools and are merely vocational, lacking the inculcation of liberalizing values. The techs have been held in some suspicion by schools, particularly where students have preferred them to the sixth form. The values are not the traditional school values; courses are traditionally available to all; the colleges are open institutions. The tech colleges' origins are in mechanics institutes and trade schools, formed to encourage understanding by working classes of their skills and social conditions, and schoolteachers often object to this, believing that education is properly unrelated to day-to-day work and wage-earning. Techs which have grown in response to demands are suspected for debasing education.

Further education has grown more haphazardly than the school system and now presents a variety of over 700 colleges and other institutions. It suffers sometimes from not being a statutory requirement upon LEAs, as primary and secondary education is; at times of economic stringency FE tends to be cut back, as it was fairly severely in 1968. There was provision for a statutory compulsory part-time education to the age of eighteen in technical colleges in the Education

Acts of both 1917 and 1944 but in this respect they were never implemented. If the regulations for the sixteen to nineteen age-group were regularized and sixth forms and colleges brought under one system it would be the first statutory provision for FE.

The further-education system has grown outside the public debate except when those aspects of industrial training which are part of it are relevant to debate about the economic situation. There is within the Labour Party, however, a straightforward political argument over further education as to whether it is second-best, mere vocational training or whether it is to be supported for offering what the people want and industrial economy needs. The Labour Party's *Labour's Programme for Britain* put to the annual conference in 1972 brought together sixteen to eighteen education in a system which could have leanings towards FE colleges more than to schools and including full-time, part-time, block-release and day-release courses. A side effect would be to reduce the academic advantages of grammar schools and former grammar schools which perpetuate their advantage even as comprehensives through academic sixth forms.

A similar debate exists with regard to polytechnics. The Labour Secretary of State for Education and Science who proposed them in 1966, Mr Anthony Crosland, established them as the pinnacle of the public system of further education as distinct from the universities. Polytechnics were to enjoy the esteem of the universities and to be institutions of higher education but their values were to be those of the technical colleges, with more vocational bias and more part-time students, and they were to be 'comprehensive academic communities'. Thus they were intended to serve the interests of working-class students and the national economy where the universities did not seem able to, particularly with regard to the former. Some elements within the Labour Party, however, unable to believe in the different values, argue that the polytechnics are merely higher education on the cheap, a second-best for the masses. Thus the encouragement of the polytechnics under Mrs Thatcher's rule was viewed with scepticism. The polytechnics, for their part, however, are busy betraying their origins and intentions by increasing academic and full-time courses and thereby attracting higher percentages of middle-class students. The blame for this can be laid at the door of inadequate Government implementation of its policy, but it illustrates once more how an expansion of education, justified by the need to extend opportunity, has in practice been used by the middle classes to maintain their advantage.

Further education is too large a subject to discuss at all properly in this book. It includes also adult education, the thousands of evening institutes and evening classes at technical colleges which are often dismissed as 'ballroom dancing and flower arrangements'; but which provide access to education for a large proportion of the adult population. This has been a much neglected field despite its potential and the example it might be able to give to other sections of education. The publication of the Russell Report[8] has turned attention in its direction, however, and a number of factors could contribute to a revival of interest among the educational establishment; in a fast-changing society skills and learning may have to be renewed at different stages of life; a package of learning assembled between five and sixteen, eighteen or twenty-one cannot be adequate for the rest of one's life; among those people who are most alienated by school are many who would welcome the chance to take further qualifications some years later – and it is for the benefit of society and its manpower as well as for the individuals that there should be provision. The Open University has contributed in this direction, having been backed forcefully by the Labour Party.

The further development of the argument for adult education, however, is owed to UNESCO and to France and to the concept of *education permanente*, translated as continued or lifetime education. It may be no more than a smarter name but it describes an education service which would be available to people throughout their lives, to use whenever appropriate, making possible much greater flexibility and reducing the dependence upon school.

4 Community schools

Within the school system and within the concept of compulsory education but breaking new ground on both is the idea of the community school. The community school associates to some measure school with community. It may only be a matter of making school-based facilities available for community use or may fully integrate school and community. The report on the educational priority areas went far in the latter form and defined the community school as 'the organization and process of learning through all of the social relationships into which an individual enters at any point in his lifetime':[9]

Thus the community school seeks almost to obliterate the boundary between school and community, to turn the community into a school and the school into a community. It emphasizes both teaching and learning roles for all social positions so that children may teach and teachers learn as well as vice versa, and parents may do both instead of neither.

The community school is not a sudden idea. In 1927 Henry Morris as director of education for Cambridgeshire had his county council accept the idea of village colleges which would provide both secondary schools and community centres. During the 1960s the idea was encouraged by two developments. The first was the realization that it was uneconomic to spend so much in sports and other recreational facilities for schools and then to leave them unused for many evenings, weekends, and school holidays. Adult education was growing with increasing numbers of adults looking for facilities for both recreational and vocational further education or, simply, leisure pursuits. It was sensible, when the relevant departments of local government could co-ordinate, to provide facilities for dual use by schools and community.

In 1965 in Nottinghamshire the director of education, Mr W. G. Lawson, and county architect, Mr Henry Swain, set up a development team to prepare plans for the county's new comprehensive schools, co-operating also with urban and rural district councils in provision of community facilities. These schools have, for example, concert halls which can be used for professional concerts, amateur music groups and dances, theatres for drama and film societies and public meetings, foyers, coffee bars and seminar rooms for meetings of local associations and parent–teacher associations, sports halls, hard floodlit playing areas and swimming pools for children and public. Other local services such as health centres, youth employment office and nursery school could be added. Several other LEAs, among them Leicestershire, Cumberland and Coventry, have developed similar schemes as community colleges in which, perhaps, youth service and further education are also combined. The DES encouraged dual use schemes in Circular 2/70 issued in 1970.

The second stimulus was the Plowden Report and the EPA project. In drawing attention to the importance of parental involvement in children's education they also pointed out the inadequacy of the opportunities for adults. The EPA schemes, working through primary schools and pre-school playgroups, saw the need to educate parents as well as children. The Liverpool EPA project, for example, encouraged parents into the schools during school hours and in the evenings to watch and talk about their children's education and to join in adult activities (chapter 10). The community school is therefore an attempt to drop the barriers between school and the community around it. The community school, in this definition, also requires community control through its managing or governing body. The community school does not consist, however, just of letting the community into the school. As developed in the EPA projects, it is concerned equally with making the education of the children relevant to the community. The children's education must be relevant not only to their experiences – and thereby engage their interest – but also to the life they will lead. Dr Eric Midwinter's report from Liverpool EPA calls this a 'social education':[10]

> [An education] that might give them the social competence to examine the depressing reality of their world, in the hope that they might learn to repair or change it in ways agreeable and pleasing to them. Through a close investigation of their social environment, the children might be that much readier to understand their own needs with clarity. From that standpoint they might come to invent ways and means of satisfying those needs.

He suggests four ground-rules for a community curriculum. It should be social rather than academic with reality-based themes. It should have a basis in the locality in centring on study of the immediate environment. It should concentrate on skills rather than information. It should involve a change of teachers' attitudes from defending the *status quo* to recognizing that an EPA area 'should be reformed and that its children, as junior citizens, should be forewarned and forearmed for the struggle'.

There are, therefore, political implications of community schools, and these are discussed in the national report on EPAs:[11]

> If we are concerned with the majority of children who will spend their lives in E.P.A.s, rather than only with the minority,

who will leave them for universities and colleges and middle class occupations elsewhere, then the schools must set out to equip their children to meet the grim reality of the social environment in which they live and to reform it in all its aspects, physical, organic, technical, cultural and moral.

It is therefore the reverse of the conventional concept of education in which the teacher attempts to initiate the child into higher values which will help lift him out of his environment. It is the reverse of the syndrome, which once dominated Labour Party thinking, of the bright working-class lad who makes his way to the top via the local grammar school. Against it there is levelled the charge that the community curriculum fails to show the higher values which might inspire a child to do something about his lot and instead encourages the child to accept the environment he has studied. The EPA proponents, whilst acknowledging this as a danger, deny it and point out, as Dr Midwinter (p. 19) does: 'One hopes to replace resignation and negative rebelliousness with a positive reformist attitude.'

5 Vouchers

The expansion of education has been in terms of state education. Education has been made free and compulsory and has been conducted in schools maintained by LEAs. But one idea which challenges this is that of 'vouchers' which would introduce a version of paying for education into the state system.

The suggestion is that at birth a child should be credited with a certain number of vouchers which he or she could cash in for various forms of education, in schools, colleges, universities and less formal organizations. The suggestions come from some interestingly different political directions.

In Britain the idea of vouchers has been most associated with right-wing advocates of freedom of choice. It may be a reaction to the discovery that some of their 'freedom of choice' has been lost in the process of going comprehensive, that they can no longer choose to send their children to grammar schools. It may be a reaction to a feeling that there is increasing state control and less opportunity for personal intervention. If parents want to opt out of the state education system, they can send their children to independent schools but then they have to pay fees, having already paid taxes to support the public education system. Thus instead of such parents having to pay twice over, vouchers could be traded in against part or all of independent school fees.

Dr Rhodes Boyson, Chairman of the National Council for Educational Standards, argued at the council's conference in January 1973 the case for vouchers on grounds of parental choice and of making schools more accountable to parents and public:[12]

> Schools have to be accountable to someone. . . . This is why I have regularly advocated the educational voucher whereby each parent receives a non-transferable voucher for each child equivalent to the cost of state education at that age and he can use this voucher to buy a place in a school of his free choice in or out of the state system. Schools would then be responsive to parents individually and collectively. . . . Schools would have to be responsive to parents or they would close and there would be a wide variety of public, state, community and private schools all catering for parental demand.

In other countries, less troubled than Britain by their independent schools as a source of inequality, vouchers have been proposed from a left-wing vantage point. One problem of universal, free education is that it makes it difficult to direct extra resources to the children who need them most. Positive discrimination applied to schools or areas benefits poor and rich children there alike. With vouchers additional credits could be given to compensate for social disadvantages. Universal free education has also tended to encourage education to form up as a solid block from five through to A-levels or university degree, and this may favour the middle class. Vouchers could provide more flexibility by offering people the choice of spending their credits on university, retraining later in life or various forms of further education which might be more useful to them.

One problem that crops up with the latter argument is that one is led to ask who is going to decide what is educational for whom. The middle-class conscience can be aroused by suggesting that schools and universities are peculiarly middle-class pursuits and often leisure pursuits. One can then be led to suggesting that vouchers should also be cashable for, say, a spell of pigeon racing, fishing or going on safari. Vouchers could well become a fashionable proposal but in itself it would be ambivalent.

6 Free schools

Free schools have attracted attention out of all proportion either to their number or to any body of theory behind them. They conflict with conventionally progressive assumptions about education and have broken the ranks of socialist educationists by being independent schools. The idea of free schools has caught the disillusion with the ability of state schools to cope, particularly with the crisis of social and educational problems in the cities.

Free schools have brought into the city environment the tradition of 'progressive schools', the independent and liberated schools of which Summerhill is the supreme example, and made it available free to under-privileged children. To a great extent free schools are a response by certain teachers to their own classroom experiences rather than to educational theories. The books of Jonathan Kozol[13] and John Holt[14] have helped crystallize teachers' experiences by reporting from American city schools on the crushing of children's spirits in conventional schools and on the frustrations and rewards of radical teachers. They reported how schools oppressed already disadvantaged children by their authoritarian manners and by their alien values, whereas children's creativity and independence could be encouraged by working from experiences which were real to them and treating them as people in their own right. This liberating spirit is supported to some extent by the writings of Ivan Illich on deschooling (see pp. 126–33) and by the example of Danish free schools and experiments in street schools in the US.

Free schools try to do what conventional schools and teachers often claim they would like to do but is impossible. Free schools would prefer to attract children to school rather than compel their attendance, to make freedom a strength rather than a weakness and to run without formal discipline and regular timetables. But whereas the conventional school sees its purpose as the maintenance of standards which are unattainable for many children, the free school – its teachers often rebels from the state system – tries first to treat the child as an individual and to adapt teaching and learning to what he can do. A school day, for example, might begin with teachers and children gathering to discuss what is to be done that day, with teachers explaining what is on offer or children saying what they would like to do. Most of the children, at least in these early days of the schools, are those children who were getting nothing out of the state schools and were truanting and troublesome, but in the free schools they have been happier and able to learn.

The free schools are therefore a voluntary intervention into the state system – all the more voluntary for the fact that teachers were not paid because of lack of funds. It is also, however significant, a small intervention, although a number of free schools were being discussed or planned. The established ones at Scotland Road, Liverpool, White Lion Street, Islington, and Kirkdale, South London, are registered or provisionally registered as independent schools. A few other groups of teachers and children are using what has become known as 'otherwise' status from the wording of the Education Act 1944 which places responsibility upon the parent to have their children educated 'by regular attendance at school or otherwise'. They work by a similar arrangement to that of parents educating their own children or having private tutors.

The extent to which local authorities and the DES accept free schools may depend not only upon how tolerant they are but also how desperate they are. Most of the children whom the schools and groups have taken are those who disrupted schools or for whom schools could do nothing. Where these schools may find official support is in helping with problems of truancy and children in trouble. Social services departments are experimenting with 'intermediate treatment centres', and although the free schools resist any attempts to be cast in these solely remedial functions it may be that any financial assistance is given for social services and community work.

7 Deschooling

Deschooling is the most alien idea to the conventional progressive concepts of British education. It doesn't call for a faster run in the same direction: we have assumed that we were progressing and that what was required was more of the same, more compulsory education, more influence of the education system on everyday lives and on the economy, more contribution of education to the skilled manpower, more university places. Deschooling looks with fear at such developments and demands the system be broken down; it makes a distinction between school and education. As such it is likely to appeal to the misgivings from the right as much as to the left, but simply as a catch-phrase it risks being counterproductive in attacking the school system without replacing it with the extensive learning systems which the proponents of deschooling envisage.

In the United Kingdom deschooling is associated with free schools, somewhat inaccurately. It seems, however, part of the same movement towards a breaking down of the rigidities of school and an encouragement of the libertarian potential of education. Ivan Illich himself dismisses the free schoolers: 'The free-school movement entices unconventional educators, but ultimately does so in support of the conventional ideology of schooling.'[15]

But it would be characteristically British to adapt his ideas to coalesce with adaptations of the free school ethos, and probably too of the community school, and to regard the whole as 'an experiment'.

Meantime, the mainstream reaction can be judged from the speech of Mr Edward Britton, General Secretary of the NUT, at the union conference in April 1972. He accused 'intellectual quislings' who opposed compulsory education after benefiting from it themselves and he linked deschoolers with the 'violence brigade' (those who exaggerated and exploited incidents of violence in schools – a swipe at the rival union, the NAS, who at that time were campaigning on this theme). 'Education is the most dangerous threat to vested interest and privilege that exists anywhere', he told the conference (*Guardian*, 4 April 1972):

> Give a boy or girl a good education and you have given them the key to a future that no one can take away from them. . . .
> It is the education system that we work for, and we, the teachers who work in it, that have given these people [those who would never have had a chance in life] a reasonable chance of a better life.

The deschoolers and other enemies of popular education were, he claimed, by casting doubt on the education service allowing the

Secretary of State for Education to get away with providing inadequate facilities and thereby hindering the work of the education system and teachers.

The theory of deschooling is propounded most notably by Ivan Illich in *Deschooling Society* and Everett Reimer in *School is Dead*.[16] As Illich writes, 'Together we have come to realize that for most men the right to learn is curtailed by the obligation to attend school.'

Their work has been focused on the Center for Intercultural Documentation in Mexico and on experience in Central America (and by links with Paulo Freire to South America), Puerto Rico and New York City. It has seen common problems in the Third World and among the deprived population of cities and has proposed similar educational solutions. In both situations attempts to compensate for social disadvantages through schooling have been unproductive, and both share analogous problems, the problems of the dispossessed and of those oppressed by the ideals of a consumer and capitalist society. One of Illich's most remarkable examples is of a huge Coca-Cola advertisement in a thirsty desert; just as the need for a drink is reified into a demand for Coca-Cola so is the need for learning reified into schools. He cites also the building of motorways in a developing country for use by the few rich when a similar amount of money could provide simple tractors for everybody.

There are two starting points for the deschoolers' criticisms. The first is that the system of schooling cannot hope to match the demand or the need for education. Compulsory school which requires school buildings, trained teachers and compulsory attendance cannot cope with the logistics of universal education. Statistics from UNESCO show that despite the massive expansion of education and the fact that the percentage of illiterates in the world has dropped (from 44·3 per cent in 1950 to 34·2 per cent in 1970), the actual number has increased from 700 million in 1950 to 783 million in 1970. By the end of the century there will still probably be 650 million. One of the explanations proposed by Illich and Reimer is the commitment to use of resources which schooling involves. Once a country is committed to schooling, it is committed to higher and university education, the culmination of the process. University education, however, if it is to be worthy of the name of 'university' is very much more expensive. The result is that the graduate of a Latin American university has 350 times as much public money spent on his education as on the citizen of median income.

Schooling in other words perpetuates the privileges of the upper classes; the provision of university places is taken up by them disproportionately to the poor.

The report *Learning to Be* from UNESCO states the problem:[17]

> With a few possible exceptions, governments are facing a dilemma. On one hand, it is or will eventually become impossible or at least irrational to mobilise financial resources in direct proportion to the total demand for schooling. On the other, the demand for education is already greater or soon will be of far greater dimensions than traditional educational systems have the capacity to handle, even when operating at optimum levels. Under these circumstances, governments can hardly fail to question whether trying to satisfy this demand uniquely through existing institutions and budgets is reasonable, and whether it would not be more appropriate to use other forms and other means.

The second starting point of the deschoolers is the nature of schooling and the way in which the institutionalization of education into schools affects people. 'The mere existence of school discourages and disables the poor from taking control of their own learning.' Writing from his experience in Central America, Reimer sees children removed from their environments and traditional life and transplanted into schools where, paradoxically, they are taught not how to succeed but what failures they are:[18]

> In 1960, half the children who entered school in Latin America never started the second grade, and half the second graders never started the third. Three-fourths dropped out before they learned to read. They did learn, however, how unsuited they were to school, how poor their clothing was, how bad their manners, how stupid they were in comparison with those who went on to higher grades.

Illich summarizes the effect:[19]

> Everywhere all children know that they were given a chance, albeit an unequal one, in an obligatory lottery, and the presumed equality of the international standard now compounds their original poverty with the self-inflicted discrimination accepted by the drop-out.

But school has also perverted the objects of learning:[20]

> The pupil is . . . 'schooled' to confuse teaching with learning, grade advancements with education, a diploma with competence and fluency with the ability to say something new.

It removes children from the educational environment of the village or city. It sets the values of the school, discrediting non-professional activity, limiting the ability of people to do things for themselves and increasing their dependence upon institutions like school. Reimer summarizes what schools do:[21]

> 1. Define the product or service which satisfies the need (e.g. schools define education as schooling).
> 2. Induce general acceptance of this definition among the needy (e.g. people are persuaded to identify education as schooling).
> 3. Exclude part of the needy population from full access to the product or service (e.g. schools, at some level, are available to only some people).
> 4. Pre-empt the resources available for satisfying the need (e.g. schools use up the resources available for education).

The privileged children whose values are those of the schools and whose homes support them are successful in school and use up more and more resources. Meanwhile, the poor or underprivileged child gets less than his share, learns he is a failure and is kept in a position of enslavement. He loses his freedom.

It is not possible to dismiss this as part of the international/UNESCO syndrome of concern for the Third World which cannot be applied to the United Kingdom. The problems are too similar. There may not be the enormous wastage of the system expressed in terms of drop-outs; there is not mass illiteracy. But there are great in-equalities, which the school system has not been able to compensate for. School is still for most people the experience of failure. The rigid institutionalization of learning into schooling has taken place. One parent commented to the teacher: 'This education isn't a good thing because my son with all the education you're giving him isn't going to have the same chances as I had without.' Increasingly advanced qualifications (exam passes) are required. The commitment to schooling operates as the deschoolers describe. Because school is accepted as a *sine qua non*, the 'best' – with the 'standards' it implies

– has to be maintained whether it is university entry (in the hope of increasing the opportunity to enter it) or the grammar school tradition at the expense of secondary moderns and comprehensives. The expansion of university places has in fact not increased their availability to the working classes any more than to the middle class. The work of Basil Bernstein, mentioned in chapter 7, is just one set of evidence as to how the values imposed by schools are alien to a large proportion of pupils. The instruments of the system have failed, and yet the solution proposed is still more of the same, which is not possible because of the cost and lack of resources. Furthermore, in times of economic stringency it is the less formal systems – further education and adult education – in which public expenditure is reduced or restrained so that schools are maintained.

Ivan Illich's comments on the lack of success of the USA's Title One programme which spent three billion dollars can be referred to the United Kingdom and to the plans made in the White Paper 1972 to expand nursery schools. There could be three possible explanations for the lack of success, writes Illich, choosing for his own the third:[22]

1. Three billion dollars are insufficient to improve the performance of six million children by a measurable amount.
2. The money was incompetently spent: different curricula, better administration, further concentration of the funds on the poor child, and more research are needed and would do the trick.
3. Educational disadvantages cannot be cured by relying on education within the school.

The structure of school means that resources cannot be concentrated on learning and on the disadvantaged child, but have to be dissipated on custodial care and on the better-off child in the same school.

It has been calculated in the USA that it would take 80 billion dollars a year to provide equal treatment for all, as compared to 36 million now, or by 1974 107 billion dollars needed as against 45 billion projected.

The solution proposed by Illich and Reimer is that the school system should be broken down so that the child is able to experience reality rather than the myths about society and values which the schools perpetuate. 'Learning webs', 'opportunity networks' should be formed through which the individual could contact learning resources, people who could teach and fellow students.

There is a third starting point for the deschoolers – educational technology. Educational technology and the use of programmed learning and teaching machines have proved the inefficiency of many other types of learning. The deschoolers would build networks out of computers, teaching machines and experts and build it into the fabric of society, forming what the UNESCO *Learning to Be* report called a 'learning society'. People would be able to learn naturally.

Reimer describes the kind of educational institutions needed as public utilities, rather like the water supply, and Illich describes them similarly as 'convivial institutions', including along with the water supply such open access systems as the (United States) telephone system and public markets. Convivial institutions are opposed to 'manipulative institutions' which, like schools, dominate and use people, and are right-wing institutions.

The great argument raised against deschooling is that it, again, might benefit only those privileged sections of society which were motivated enough and rich enough to make use of the learning networks. The middle-class child would be taught to read by his mother whereas the working-class child would be ignored. In other words, children have to be compelled to go to school in their own best interests. This actually takes us back to the deschoolers' argument – that school is predominantly a custodial institution.

There is, too, the fear that it is all too much like romantic capitalism and a faith in free markets. The hope, however, is that it is revolutionary liberation. There are therefore very profound political consequences as well as the left-wing motivation. People would no longer be manipulated by schools; the working class and the oppressed would no longer be dominated by the values of the ruling class and of the consumer and capitalist (and state communist) society. Illich writes:[23]

> I believe that a desirable future depends on our deliberately choosing a life of action over a life of consumption, on our engendering a life style which will enable us to be spontaneous, independent, yet related to each other, rather than maintaining a life style which only allows us to make and unmake, produce and consume – a style of life which is merely a way station of

the road to the depletion and pollution of the environment. The future depends more upon our choice of institutions which support a life of action than on our developing new ideologies and technologies.

8 The learning society

In 1972 UNESCO published a report which brought into focus radical criticisms of existing education systems throughout the world. Produced by the International Commission on the Development of Education, presided over by Edgar Faure, and entitled *Learning to Be*, it assessed these criticisms and turned them into proposals for reforms. It envisaged for the future a 'learning society'.

Taking as its starting point evidence like that presented by the deschoolers, the report argued that 'linear expansion' of education systems (that is, more of the same) would be inadequate to provide democratic education systems in which all people had true equality of opportunity. There had to be alternative strategies, radical changes from existing systems, and, persuaded by the efficacy of educational technology in providing individual instruction, it defined education in terms not of what schools provide but what individuals, each differently, need. It identified developments in education which should be encouraged by reforming the institutions:[24]

> The act of teaching gives way to the act of learning. While not ceasing to be taught, the individual becomes less of an object and more of a subject. He does not receive education as if it were a gift or a social service handed out to him by his guardians, the powers-that-be. He assimilates it by conquering knowledge and himself, which makes him supreme master and not the recipient of acquired knowledge.

In beginning with the individual it produces a different definition for equality of opportunity. It does not mean equal facilities or equal opportunity to enter educational institutions:[25]

> Equal opportunity for all does not mean nominal equality, the same treatment for everyone, as many still believe today; it

means making certain that each individual receives a suitable education at a pace and through methods adapted to his particular person.

Education must be available for people whenever they need it; there must be 'lifelong education' – a development of the concepts of continued or recurrent education – and this would be 'the keystone of the learning society'. As a principle on which the education system is founded, lifelong education recognizes that in a fast-changing society people need retraining or up-dating at various times in their lives. It is intended also to break through all the restrictions and barriers to education imposed by selection and examination procedures:[26]

> Once education becomes continual, ideas as to what constitutes success and failure will change. An individual who fails at a given age and level in the course of his educational career will have other opportunities. He will no longer be relegated for life to the ghetto of his own failure.

And this would be a more democratic education system because existing selection and exams, through meritocratic rather than aristocratic, still are biased to particular kinds of ability and by social class. There would be a diversity of institutions without barriers, with open access.

Democracy is not achieved just by providing equality of opportunity, for education is also 'an essential factor in shaping the future' and at least has to prepare mankind to adapt to changes – 'to create a dynamic, non-conformist, non-conservative frame of mind'. The learning society is dedicated to reform, and the report takes its cue from the work of Paulo Freire,[27] for whom 'a humanizing pedagogy' is an essential instrument of revolution. He has developed a concept of 'conscientization'. which is defined as 'learning to perceive social, political, and economic contradictions, and to take action against the oppressive elements of reality'. Teachers and students together would be engaged in 'unveiling' reality and acting upon it, and the teacher's role would be – indeed, has been in Freire's teaching in South America – that of creating a dialogue with oppressed people. For revolutionary purposes, education must not be imposed but must develop from people's wants:[28]

This view of education starts with the conviction that it cannot present its own programme but must search for this programme dialogically with the people, it serves to introduce the pedagogy of the oppressed, in the development of which the oppressed must participate.

This chapter has discussed different relationships of school and society, whether conceived as community schools or the learning society. There should be an integration of learning institutions into society. Whereas schools have made a virtue of being closed institutions and separate from society – a preparation for life – these various proposals seek to provide learning institutions which are open, both in terms of entry and in relations with other social activities. Similarly, the kind of learning is not of authority and standards in subjects but of critical examination of society and environment, not so much of knowledge but of competence. The proposals are in different ways positively reformist. Schools have been an instrument of social reform but in an indirect fashion in so far as they have sought to improve people and society, whereas these proposals have formed a direct relationship between learning in school and action outside it.

There are obviously difficulties in translating the Faure Report, *Learning to Be*, from the international scene to England and Wales, not least of which for the pragmatic and muddled English is its idealism, but the ideas correspond in some ways: lifelong education and its diversity of institutions correspond to the development of further and adult education; a reformist approach to learning corresponds to the curricula suggested for the community schools. The learning society as an overall concept bears more relationship to post-school than to school education, although a more complete and more available post-school education system would reduce people's need to gather all their education in school and university. The Labour Party's Opposition Green Paper on *Higher and Further Education*, published in January 1973, sought likewise to open access to adult education (chapter 1.1). In February 1973 the report of the Ontario Commission of Post-Secondary Education called its report *The Learning Society* and proposed 'universal access' not only to existing institutions but also to less structured forms of education outside the regular system.

The political implications of these proposals are twofold. First, they are dedicated to reforming society, and as such would have to test their success or failure not by the traditional assessments of the education service like success in university entry but by the changes they had produced in society. Second, they are not only democratic in their intentions for society but in their operation in schools, other institutions and administration. They would not only involve during the introduction of the reforms a questioning of established authority but also continuing involvement by students and learners in decisions about the government and administration of education. The concepts of learning, the forms of organizations and the methods of control are interdependent.

References

1 *Statistics of Education, 1971, vol. 5, Finance and Awards*, HMSO, London, 1972.
2 Robbins Report: *Higher Education*, HMSO, London, 1963.
3 *Education: A Framework for Expansion* (White Paper), HMSO, London, 1972.
4 *Statistics of Education, vol. 1, Schools*, HMSO, London, 1972.
5 J. W. B. Douglas, J. M. Ross and H. R. Simpson, *All Our Future*, Peter Davies, London, 1968, p. 25.
6 Crowther Report: *15 to 18*, HMSO, London, 1959, pp. 108 and 116.
7 Ibid., p. 123.
8 Russell Report: *Adult Education: A Plan for Development*, HMSO, 1973.
9 A. H. Halsey, *Educational Priority: EPA Problems and Policies*, vol. 1, HMSO, London, 1972, p. 189.
10 E. Midwinter, *Priority Education*, Penguin, Harmondsworth, 1972, p. 19.
11 Halsey, op. cit., p. 117.
12 Quoted in *The Accountability of Schools*, Churchill Press, Enfiled, 1973.
13 J. Kozol, *Death at an Early Age*, Penguin, Harmondsworth, 1968.
14 J. Holt, *The Underachieving School*, Penguin, Harmondsworth, 1971.
15 I. D. Illich, *Deschooling Society*, Calder & Boyars, London, 1971, p. 65.
16 E. Reimer, *School is Dead*, Penguin, Harmondsworth, 1971.
17 E. Faure et al., *Learning to Be*, UNESCO, Paris; Harrap, Enfield, 1972, p. 48.
18 Reimer, op. cit., p. 17.
19 Illich, op. cit., p. 44.
20 Ibid., p. 1.
21 Reimer, op. cit., p. 68.
22 Illich, op. cit., p. 5.
23 Ibid., p. 52.
24 E. Faure et al., op. cit., p. 161.
25 Ibid., p. 75.
26 Ibid., p. 77.
27 P. Freire, *Pedagogy of the Oppressed*, Penguin, Harmondsworth, 1972.
28 Ibid., p. 95.

Part three

Power and participation

9 The demands for democracy

1 Protest

The first two parts of this book described the political workings of the school system and some of the political issues which concern schools, and we saw ways in which these were interdependent. In this third part we discuss a more severe political contest which although about the operation of the system has implications for the kind of education provided in schools. Protest actions by students, teachers and parents have disturbed the operation of the education system and have, coupled with demands for participation, challenged its distribution of power and many of the assumptions on which it is based.

Many protest actions are in themselves short-lived and insignificant – a quickly forgotten petition, disruption of a public meeting, one or two children withdrawn from school – but as part of a phenomenon they strike at the foundations of the system. The effect of protests, small and large, is all the more shattering to those individuals in authority at whom they are directed because of the conviction those individuals have of the essential rightness of what they are doing. A headteacher does not doubt he is acting in the interests of the children. The protests are shattering, too, because the school system is presumed to be working for the good of everyone. A local education office works devotedly at giving the children in its area a decent education within the available resources. Often therefore protests seem to these individuals to be personally malicious and to the administration to be destructive or counter-productive, regardless of the arguments.

The education system, as we have seen, has many ways in which it tries to work in the best interests of everyone. At different levels of policy-making and administration there are processes of consultation and checks or balances on powers. The problem is not therefore of unbridled use of power but of the way in which education is run through administrative measures out of public view

– even when the issues are political – and through individual professional judgments. It is therefore difficult to argue issues other than in
the set framework, and the importance of securing adequate resources for the education service adds to an emphasis on not rocking
the boat. The conviction of the service as a whole and of teachers
and administrators that they are working for the good of everybody
makes them intolerant of criticisms, whilst the weight attached to
their professional individual judgment encourages them to see
criticisms and complaints as personally malicious. To kick up a row
in public is in the context in which education operates not just an
embarrassment but a threat.

But kicking up a row in public is what has been done. The way
the education system operates depends upon its acceptance by those
for whom it is provided, but what has happened is that either in
individual cases or in general matters some of those people have
ceased to trust it. When a headteacher or administrator has asserted
that something is in the general interest, he has been accused of
acting out of his selfish bureaucratic convenience or of arbitrarily
acting against certain individuals. The paternal authority of the
education service finds it difficult to answer such accusations
because it believes in avoiding public controversy in the interests of
promoting its subtle, liberal values. It has not, moreover, consulted
those for whom education is provided – parents, students or children
– partly because it mistrusts what it believes they would interpret
as their own interests. Teachers often think of themselves as fighting
against the selfish values of children and the acquisitive aspirations
of their parents.

There are different reasons for this breakdown in trust and the
refusal to accept the established authority. Almost invariably the
protests begin with a specific allegation of injustice and then, if they
are given time and thought to develop, are related to wider issues.
Whilst there is almost always an element of self-interest, there are
different ways in which the wider issues are involved, as the parent
power movements show (chapter 10). The outcome is generally
demands for representation or participation and democracy, for
democracy in some form.

The most dramatic protests were the student rebellions in the
London School of Economics, Hornsey and Guildford School of
Art, Essex, Birmingham and many other universities since the hectic,
almost revolutionary year of 1968. The sit-ins and other protests

have become a regular part of student action, for example, in recent years at Lancaster University and the Polytechnic of North London. Student protest proved to be the vanguard of other actions rather than isolated and temporary phenomena. Industrial workers have used sit-ins and work-ins to put their case and to keep their works open after threats of closure, Upper Clyde Shipbuilders most notably. By example parents have become more militant in support of campaigns for their children's education and the school kids themselves have adopted such tactics. The protests have all been part of a rising tide of demonstrations against home and foreign policies.

The student rebellions help explain the factors involved in other protests. Decisions made by hierarchical authority, such as vice-chancellor or headteacher, have not been accepted by the people on whom they have been imposed. The decision may have been blatantly unjust and therefore prompted reaction, but equally the protest may result from the way the decision was reached and therefore is an indication of people's different levels of tolerance in what they will accept. In the early 1960s students, unions accepted that informal and private chats between their president and the vice-chancellor were the appropriate way of representing their opinions. Typically what happened then was that a particular case or series of cases created controversy and that with the object of clearing things up – presuming that their authority would be accepted – the vice-chancellor or professors issued some form of ultimatum. Instead of the vice-chancellor's word being accepted his action was taken to increase the injustice; when authority was challenged it reacted illiberally in order to protect itself. There would then be a confrontation, perhaps a sit-in or other trial of strength or demonstration of feeling. It was difficult for people with personal authority not only to consider opposing arguments, but also, structurally, it was difficult to cope with attitudes or opinions which challenged their right to be powerful. Even to talk man to man or representative to representative could seem to reduce their own authority by acknowledging that the other side had some validity. Student protest also mapped out the forms of protest which were available and extended the opportunities of protesters to react publicly and strongly. The sight and the success of a mass sit-in or a demonstration showed that it was possible to take protest further than a letter and an angry phone-call. Ordinary respectable mothers and fathers became prepared to take part in more militant forms of protest.

2 On the inside: Teachers

Universities responded to the student troubles by making arrangements for students to be represented on advisory and decision-making committees. Students have also gained representation on the boards of governors and, less often, academic boards of technical colleges and colleges of education. The vigour of student demands assisted junior staff in universities and teachers in colleges to get a larger say in the government of their institutions, breaking the monopoly of power held in universities by professors and in colleges by the principal.

A major operation of reforming the government of technical colleges and colleges of education was undertaken by the DES and LEAS in the late 1960s and first years of the 1970s. It began with the Weaver Report[1] which in 1966 proposed that boards of governors should be established for colleges and given certain autonomous powers as a means of making the colleges more independent of local authorities and of giving teachers more control over academic matters. The Weaver Report was actually established not so much with democratic intentions as to resolve the frustrations reported from the colleges with local authority management and the disappointment of the colleges of education at not being allowed to join up with the – autonomous – universities as the Robbins Report had suggested. In the event, however, these issues became wrapped up with the demands of teachers and students for representation.

When the polytechnics were being established from 1966 onwards, the DES and the Labour ministers of education, particularly Mrs Shirley Williams, insisted that they had instruments and articles of government which not only established boards of governors with democratic representation of staff but also academic boards by which staff should have decision-making powers on academic matters and which would comprise heads of department and elected teacher representatives. The arguments for academic boards were couched partly in terms of democracy and participation but rather more in terms of the greater efficiency of devolving reponsibilities to teachers and of the recognition of polytechnic teachers' professional status. The DES insisted also that students be represented on governing bodies and that their rights in disciplinary procedures be written into articles of government. From the polytechnics, these reforms were then carried in to other technical and further education colleges under the guidance given by the DES in Circular 7/70.

A similar movement could be anticipated in schools, and the main teachers' unions have debated the issues. The HMA in its 1972 statement on *The Government of Schools*, discussed in chapter 5, rejected the application of ideas imported from higher and further education and insisted that, whilst consultations were valuable, the headteacher had to retain his authority. The NAS, however, in its statement, *Thoughts on a New Education Act*, in 1970, recommended that schools should be required to have academic boards to which the headteacher as its chairman and chief executive would be accountable.

The centre of the debate is within the NUT, the argument ranging from its left-wing Rank and File's proposals for democratic running of schools to its Executive's headteacherly caution. A working party of the NUT reported in autumn 1972 and recommended that the union promote teacher participation by suggesting that the DES revise its model articles of government for schools and by urging its case upon the LEAS. The working party argued that most aspects of a school's organization and structure could be a matter for collective decisions by staff and headteacher, and suggested that the role of headteacher should become that of chief executive. This, however, was too much for the union's Executive which proposed steps should be taken to make consultation mandatory.

The arguments therefore revolve around the concepts of participation or consultation. The NUT's working party summarized the difference:[2]

> With consultation there is no alteration in the basic distribution of responsibility within the school – the Head Teacher and others in executive positions would retain their present responsibilities but would exercise them in the light of the views expressed by their colleagues. With participation the Head Teacher and others in executive positions would be expected to accept the decisions of the staff in agreed areas

143

(in which they would have participated together with their colleagues) and would have the responsibility for carrying these decisions into effect.

In everyday affairs it might be hard to tell the difference between a headteacher who has retained his authority but takes consultation seriously and a headteacher who is carrying out a collective decision, but there is a fundamental difference which is revealed in crisis situations and in the forms of future development possible. It is different in two respects, in the kinds of actions that can be taken and in the nature of responsibility. An autocratic headteacher at the crunch or over a crucial issue affecting the development of his school will ultimately have to make up his own mind, act upon it and take praise or blame. What headteachers or principals of colleges who have been used to an autocratic role, with or without consultation, find difficult to understand is that the alternatives of collective decision-making imply also collective responsibility, and there should be no basis for their frequently expressed worry that they would have to carry the can for an action with which they did not agree.

The arguments over consultation or participation tend to be political in that they are concerned with democratic or other convictions and with the logic of consultation without power or control without responsibility. The basic justifications for each, however, are similar. They include that of modern practice in schools by which more responsibility for teaching is devolved to teachers and by which teachers work together in integrated studies, group teaching and so on. They include that of management practice and the increasing complexity of school organization – a development which has given rise in a few isolated instances to the appointment of a warden or administrative head rather than a conventional headteacher. There is also the argument that consultation or participation is a requisite of true professional status for teachers.

The question of participation is contentious still but that of teacher representation on governing bodies more widely accepted. The HMA, NAS and NUT are all agreed on this, and so too is the Association of Education Committees. Together with representation of parents, the cause has been accepted by many LEAS in drawing up new instruments of government for their schools.

The interests of parents and teachers are not by any means

identical, despite the ease with which their causes are linked in discussion of demands for greater democracy and for representation on governing bodies. The NUT's working party rejected the idea of consulting parents about the aims of the school:[3]

> We believe that determination of the school's educational aim should be the responsibility of the staff. But having determined those aims we believe the staff of a school should ensure that parents are fully informed and that opportunity is provided for discussion with parents of their decisions.

If this was implemented, it would not make much difference to parents whether headteacher or teachers ran the school. The problem, as discussed in the next two chapters, is of reconciling the different interests of parents and teachers.

Teachers, however, can gain greater democracy in schools not only through structures of government. In the polytechnics and technical colleges a powerful stimulus has been the requirements of the Council for National Academic Awards, which insists, when validating degree and diploma courses, that staff have shared in planning them. Similarly, the introduction of the Mode III of the CSE enables teachers to devise their own courses, which is a very different thing politically from having to accept syllabuses handed down by external examination boards and, as discussed in chapter 7, is a further element in the challenge to established authority.

3 On the inside: Students

School students, too, have demanded representation and recognition of their rights. A variety of organizations have been formed to press their opinions, most substantially the National Union of School Students and the Schools Action Union but also a variety of bodies such as Rebel, the Youth Action Kommittee (YAK), the Schools Mass Action Collective for Kids (SMACK) and local groups. Some of these bodies are transitory but the phenomenon is not. SAU was first formed in 1968 and in 1969 was claiming about 3,500 members based on forty area groups. The SAU reformed itself into a smaller organization concentrating on more sectarian and militant action, and by 1973 the NUSS had become the largest group. After a year or so it had a membership of 6,000 and expected to increase up to 20,000. Some of the actions organized by these bodies have been large. In May 1972 the SAU organized strikes and demonstrations in London schools which involved thousands of students. At the beginning of the month a few hundred marched to County Hall and in a letter to the ILEA demanded no uniforms, no caning and no detention and for rules to be decided and enforced by the whole school. They added that they would no longer 'passively accept being pushed around, beaten and locked up on the sole authority of the Head'. On 17 May the SAU with some help from NUSS organized a demonstration estimated at 4,000 strong.

The NUSS is, at the time of writing, the most organized and largest of the groups, its establishment having been helped by the NUS. It has a full-time president, an office and secretarial assistance, an organization of school and area branches with a national executive committee of twenty and cheap travel facilities. It reckons to be broadly based left-wing and has a set of policies drawn up at national conferences across the range of student rights and representation. It is committed on over two dozen issues including co-educational comprehensive schools, increased expenditure on schools, the abolition of religious education, better sex education and free state nursery schools. More specifically its policy statement (1972) includes:

> To promote greater democracy inside schools eventually leading to school committees of teachers, students, parents and non-academic staff subject to instant recall and representatives of the local community controlling the schools and organizing the curriculums.
> To work towards:
> (a) The speedy abolition of corporal punishment and the prefect system, and to encourage an increase of student responsibility and self discipline in schools.
> (b) All forms of discipline to be under the control of a school committee and all school rules to be published.
> To fight for freedom of speech, assembly and the end of censorship of school magazines, clubs and societies and the banning of non-academic and confidential files in schools, and that students be allowed to see any reference about themselves

one blemmage as study of N.U.S.S.

sent to further education establishments or prospective employers.

The NUSS policy envisages committees to run schools eventually but it is prepared to use more representative governing bodies including students in the short term. Governing bodies are suspect as being identified with the existing authoritarian system. The union has warned headteachers that school students are not to be treated like 'second-class citizens' and that they would strike if schools were not made more democratic.

The principal means through which student representation has been introduced into schools is by setting up school councils. These have provided a way of consulting and sounding out student – and, in some cases, staff – opinion. With rare exceptions, such as Countesthorpe College, the headteacher reserves his ultimate authority and the school council is not properly decision-making. The questions which school councils are most likely to deal with concern uniform, length of hair and discipline. School councils are not usually expected to discuss curriculum on the assumption that this is a professional matter for teachers.

The major problem is the relationship between the headteacher with his individual authority and the school council. The council simply by being there reduces his ability to act on his personal initiative and may be a serious challenge to his authority and to that of his staff. As we discussed in chapter 5, the headteacher assumes individual responsibility for the school, for 'his school'. It is not possible for students to set up a school council without the consent of the headteacher, though it may be possible to organize and demonstrate so that he is given little choice. Even with a school council established, however, the headteacher has so much individual authority and control of the administrative processes that it is not difficult either to delay or to ignore proposals. He also has severe sanctions available – expulsion, caning, suspension – against unilateral action by students. The individual headteacher may be prepared to allow school council decisions to be implemented unless he considers them damaging or he may allow the council only to offer him advice. There is wide discretion available to the headteacher as to what is damaging or against school interests. He may consider that absolute adherence to school uniform is an essential element of school spirit and discipline. It is very radical to suggest

147

that students either do know best or have the right to decide. Given the existing structures in which heads have autocratic powers but prefer to gain the consent of their staff, the head is likely to consult staff on proposals from the school council but he is likely to do this privately or at least so that the school council is not publicly involved. Thus not only does he retain the power to make the decision, he also controls the information.

The NFER published a report in 1970 on the organization of fifty-nine comprehensive schools,[4] which by being recently established might be expected to be more progressive than most. Half of them had school councils, but there was little evidence that students were involved in making school policy; the councils just gave pupils the chance to raise matters. Many other reports from schools suggest that students are disillusioned with existing school councils in that they seem to degenerate into talking-shops which the headteacher finds it easy to obviate.

In its statement on *The Government of Schools* in August 1972 the HMA recognized that pupils should 'be encouraged to express their opinions in schools councils or in less formal settings'. It continued:

> We do not believe that they should control their own schools.
> We see no useful purpose in any national organization of school
> students and we regard as foolish in the extreme the activities
> of a few pupils who have demonstrated and attempted the
> organization of strikes against school rules and the authority
> of headmasters and teachers. Such activities are antipathetic
> to the purposes of education.

The mere fact that demands are made by school students – as well as the demands themselves – is radical in challenging the authority of the headteacher. It shows, for example, that school students do not accept the underlying 'them–us' attitude of teachers by which education is conceived as telling children what they should know rather than helping them learn it for themselves. It shows that they do not accept the power given to teachers as expressed in corporal punishment. It accuses the head of being a dictator. However, a school council or other consultative procedures may be introduced with not so much concern for the nature of authority in the school. It can be argued that experience on representative bodies and in making decisions is a useful aspect of education. It can be argued that consultation and sounding out of opinions simply make sure that what the headteacher or his staff were going to do is agreeable to all and that the procedures therefore make the school that much more efficient and happy as an organization. Against these less radical justifications, it can be argued that they represent collaboration which merely helps perpetuate existing power structures – on a less theoretical level, there have been problems in universities when students have found that what they thought were bodies which offered them a real say in decisions could be overridden or ignored by the authorities.

This discussion has been concerned mostly with the rights of students in school to representation but another facet of the problem of schools is often linked to it. It is another problem of pupil–teacher relations, another aspect of treating students with respect. This problem is that of truancy and violence, being seen together as expression of frustration, boredom and anger with schools. As we have discussed in other chapters, schools have not been effective in providing education for all their students, curricula have been irrelevant, schools have not compensated for social disadvantages, schools have perpetuated social differences. Thus not only do schools exist on the basis of telling children what to do – educationally and in discipline – but they are also wrong about it, and the consciousness of this leads some students to stay away or to break the place up.

Two interrelated responses to the problem – radical as opposed to the demand for tougher discipline – are the demands for greater democracy in schools and the assertion of children's rights. Democratic schools would, in theory, form their education out of the demands of students and would count students, intelligent or unintelligent, noisy or quiet, as members of a community along with teachers. The ACE has drafted a charter of children's rights including things like food, sleep, privacy and space to play in as well as freedom from physical punishment. The National Council for Civil Liberties has also taken up the cause of children's rights. It organized a conference in conjunction with the London Co-operative Society in March 1972 and at its council meeting in April 1972 called for a campaign on three issues – abolition of corporal punishment, the right of children to determine their personal appearance and the need for effective channels of participation by children in running the schools. The NUT has opposed the NCCL's concept of children's rights. Its representative at the NCCL conference in March 1972, executive member Jack Chambers, said that these arguments were anti-educational. The ideas did not take account of progressive developments in schools and of child-centred and broadening curricula. They attacked compulsory schooling in such a way as to give sustenance to right-wing reactionaries and to hinder the spread of equality of opportunity. Mr Chambers included among his rights for children the right 'to be protected from the possible consequences arising from the activities of those mistaken adults who, knowing little child-development, present children with too-advanced "conflict" situations and impose unfair, and potentially harmful, choices and stresses upon them'.

The HMA's statement on *The Government of Schools* reflected the same attitudes when it rejected the NCCL's idea of children's rights: 'We believe that children and adolescents need security as well as freedom and that we shall serve them ill if we do not insist upon their compliance with standards of work and behaviour the reasonableness of which must in the end be judged by adults.' But this certainty of what constitutes education and confidence in the progressive values of the education service was rejected by an SAU speaker, Simon Steyne, at the NCCL conference:

> Most of us find our education boring and irrelevant. The view of the world that our schools indoctrinate us with is not the ideology of the working people. It is the ideology of the bosses. Our schools preach mysticism, defeatism and racism and impress on us a decadent consumer culture.

References

1 Weaver Report: *The Government of Colleges of Education*, HMSO, London, 1966.
2 Appendix to *Teacher Participation*, a statement and recommendations presented by the Executive of the NUT to the annual conference, 1973, p. 10.
3 Ibid., p. 12.
4 *Comprehensive Education in Action*, NFER, Slough, 1970.

10 Politics, people and the community

1 Parent power

There seems to be hardly a local newspaper without a story of parents protesting against part of the education system. It might be an individual parent keeping his child away from school because the local authority has not offered a place in the school of his choice. Perhaps the local authority's choice of school is further from home or has not got such a good reputation or, even more idiosyncratically, is further from the primary school to which big sister has to walk her little brother. In the summer of 1972 Mr Kenneth Sibley went to prison rather than pay a £10 fine imposed for his refusal to send his daughters to a comprehensive school. The fervour of organized group protest was hotted up during 1972 by the parents' campaign with the ILEA on 11-plus transfer when parents took a leaf out of the book of student protest.

It is the 11-plus which has been the main point of controversy and action. In many LEAS parents and public debated the scheme for their area, in public meetings, newspaper columns and associations. As Robin Pedley says,[1] Circular 10/65 by requesting LEAS to submit schemes, 'sparked off a tremendous democratic debate': 'Never before can there have been so many public meetings, so many little working parties, so many inches of correspondence columns in the local and national press, devoted to education.'

Some groups of parents took the initiative in working out plans for their areas; others rallied to support or protest against the scheme proposed by the education committee. LEAS consciously tried to involve parents in discussion of the plans, as Circular 10/65 had hoped they would. The Conservative Secretary of State, Mrs Margaret Thatcher, paid much attention to local objections to comprehensive schemes. In 1972 she told the Conservative Party conference that she had upheld ninety-two of these objections 'mostly in favour of famous or well-known grammar schools' and encouraged her audience: 'I can only express the hope that those who believe intensely in the future of grammar schools and what they have to offer will be as vocal in their own areas and outside this conference hall as they are today.' Her statements stimulated local groups both pro- and anti-comprehensive. In Birmingham in 1972 more than a million signatures (many people signed several times for different schools) were collected to save the grammar schools of the city from becoming comprehensive. In Buckinghamshire rival groups campaigned so effectively that the county council made some areas comprehensive and others not. There the STEP demonstrations included an all-night vigil which gained publicity by dispersing only for the morning's Remembrance Day service. In Surrey STEP groups handed out 11-plus questions in advance and circulated leaflets explaining how selection processes actually worked, whilst the grammar school lobby collected signatures and successfully put objections to the Secretary of State to save certain schools.

There have been equally strong protests at the operation of comprehensive schemes, particularly in parents' complaints of insufficient freedom of choice over the comprehensive to which their child goes. In the ILEA in 1972 parent groups organized a series of local protest meetings culminating in locking themselves in with the chairman of the schools subcommittee and in chaining a few of their number to the railings of County Hall. The ILEA had attempted to ensure that each of its comprehensives had a fair spread of ability by reducing some of the elements of parental choice: with a completely free choice the more competent and articulate parents chose schools with a better reputation, which in turn magnified the differences between those schools and those to which only children whose parents were incompetent or disinterested went. There were therefore a few hundred parents who found their bright children had been allocated to schools which lacked a good reputation and perhaps academic facilities, and some of these withdrew their children and organized protests with some success. The potential conflict remains nevertheless between an authority believing it is acting for the benefit of the majority and the underprivileged, and parents refusing to let their children suffer. The ILEA, in fact, unintentionally helped the parent protests by inviting parents with individual protests to visit the local education offices at the same time – there they met others and organized into protest groups.

Other groups of parents have protested about inadequate buildings and facilities. In Brighton in spring 1972 parents lobbied councillors and withheld their children from school in protest against overcrowding, and persuaded the education committee to switch £1 million from building an extension for the technical college to improving primary and secondary schools. However, when the local MP asked in the House of Commons for the Government to allow this transfer, it was rejected. Later in the same year parents and pupils of Canonbury primary school demonstrated and went on strike over a reduction in teaching staff, and the ILEA agreed to supply another teacher as part of a general improvement.

At national level the campaign for increased nursery school and playgroup provision relied on parent support for their work and their presence on demonstrations. The campaign had the advantage of photogenic toddlers lobbying the Houses of Parliament. Pressure groups like CASE and NEA have co-ordinated local groups and provided a platform for parents' opinions and demands for rights. Attempts to form one massive parents' organization have, however, foundered on the different interests involved, as the story of the Home and School Council illustrates.

Individual protests and complaints all add up with the growth of pressure groups, nationally and locally, to demands for parents and their wishes to be considered to a greater extent than ever before in educational administration. The idea of 'parent power' encompasses a number of different ways of meeting these demands: more information about schools, freedom in choosing schools, PTAs, representation on governing bodies, community participation. These have different effects, but the force of the arguments are usually brought together as a demand to be involved.

The educational arguments for greater parent involvement are usually brought to the fore, though social and political arguments are as strong. The Plowden Report[2] was the watershed. One parent leader reported that when she visited the annual North of England educational conference in 1967 before the publication of the report she found that parents were a dirty word, something to be kept out of the way, but that the next year it was as though a new phenomenon had been discovered – now parents were accepted. Plowden pulled together arguments about social deprivation, social class and parental interest in education and correlated them with the child's performance in school:[3]

Educational policy should explicitly recognize the power of the environment upon the school and of the school upon the environment. Teachers are linked to parents by the children for whom they are both responsible. The triangle should be completed and a more direct relationship established between teachers and parents. They should become partners in more than name; their responsibility become joint instead of several. . . . The higher the socio-economic group, the more parents attended open days, concerts and parent-teacher association meetings, and the more often they talked with heads and class teachers. . . . Not surprisingly, less help with school work was given at home to children of manual workers. Considerably lower proportions of parents from manual worker homes bought, for use at home, copies of some of the books children were using at school. Two-thirds of unskilled workers had five books or fewer in the home, apart from children's books and magazines, as contrasted with one-twentieth of professional workers.

Eric Midwinter in his account of the Liverpool EPA project, set up as a result of Plowden's recommendations, commented on the success of establishing improved parent–teacher relations:[4]

Many teachers seem to me now to be convinced of the vital necessity for strong and supportive home relationships. . . . The justification is initially educational. The aim is to augment the educational understanding of the parents and the social understanding of the teacher, so that a closer partnership for the education of the children might be realized.

From such experience have developed the concepts of community schools, discussed in chapter 8.

But the arguments are not just educational. It is not possible to separate the demands for parent participation from other protest movements and demands for participation. Local residents have formed associations and demanded to be heard when government decisions or property speculation threaten their areas. Minority and underprivileged groups as various as women's lib, squatters and claimants' unions have shown up inadequacies and injustices in central and local government administration. Furthermore, the lack of respect for individual rights now affects not only the inarticulate and downtrodden but also those able to protest. The middle classes, whose position in society used to protect them, have been goaded into action by bureaucratic or capitalist decisions as these have become more indiscriminate or fairer and afflicted all classes more equally.

There has grown up at the same time a faith in more local forms of organization, less bureaucratic and less sophisticated. Local groups have established neighbourhood councils and looked to them to provide the democracy and concern for their problems which local councils may lack. Although a local council is fairly elected, its ballots scrupulous and its organization proper, the machinery of power works against some particular problems and local needs. In urban situations the value of 'the street' as a logical and human form of organization and community has been developed, pointing to existing local government institutions, including schools, as irrelevant or hostile.

Whatever other arguments or justifications are offered for the parent movement, one thing is clear: it shows that parents no longer are prepared to view the public education service as a charity or dole. Their readiness to complain and campaign reveals an attitude that education is a service which people are entitled to, entitled to use and entitled to expect value from. The background to such attitudes may be seen in terms of the consumer movement or participatory and grass-roots democracy, and although both can at present be lumped together as 'parent power' there is a potential conflict between them. The consumer movement, based in middle-class affluence and self-confidence, may be satisfied with good service. It will expect thorough information and guidance on choices in the education system. It will expect a defined procedure for making complaints and appeals. It will be particularly concerned with freedom of choice in schools and with gaining the best for its children, and, though it may produce benefits for all society by its pressures, it is in essence self-centred.

Should the basis be in participatory democracy, however, the demand will be for many of the same qualities in the service, but these alone would not be satisfying. Such a basis demands that parents are incorporated in the decision-making machinery. Perhaps the common statement of 'parent power' – 'I believe I have the right to say what happens to my child' – takes something from both consumerism and grass-roots democracy, but it will be interesting to see how these forces divide when parent power is established and has the chance to achieve its real objectives.

2 The issues

There will always be protests and complaints about any service, and sometimes they will score famous victories and sometimes they will come to nothing. Recent events have not, however, just been isolated cases but have consistent themes and organization through the various pressure groups. The DES and many local authorities have recognized that the parents' movement has to be considered but its demands are far from being met. What are the different issues and what is to be done about them?

The most basic and widespread theme is simply the reaction to the feeling of being shut out of the schools and education service and is expressed, fairly vaguely, as demands for more information and demands to be consulted. Superficially the demand for information could be easily met by local authorities through the common techniques of public relations – booklets of information, accounts of new proposals published in the local press, helpful answering of telephone queries. There is, as was discussed in chapter 4, an enormous demand for information about schools and about education, some of which in some localities parents' groups are helping to supply. Some local authorities, which a decade ago would have thought it improper to publish more than the name and address of the school, now provide information about curricula and other activities in different schools. The majority attempt to be co-operative in dealing with parents' queries, but are restricted by other demands on their time and resources. 'Education shops' or advice centres have proved helpful in offering information on general problems and referring specific questions to the relevant authorities, and these have been run by education authorities as well as local parents' groups and with the encouragement of the ACE. The problem, however, is that providing information may be satisfactory in some cases in itself – a parent may be unnecessarily worried or may simply wonder what is happening to the children – but may be useless unless it is possible to act upon – information about different schools is useless unless the parent can choose between them.

Likewise, to publish plans in advance and to collect the opinions of parents and public requires that they are acted upon in full or in part. In this area, as well, LEAs have made great strides forward, e.g. the ILEA's consultations with local residents during 1972 and 1973 by publishing Green Papers and holding meetings when reorganizing the patterns of local provision, and many authorities sound out local opinion in less organized ways – though some of them think they are more successful in interpreting parents' wishes than the parents themselves may think. Notice has been taken of parents' pressure groups in comprehensive reorganization at both national and local level. Groups of STEP and CASE have kept the issues before the public and pressured councillors and education officers, whilst other groups have objected to schemes.

The results of these forms of pressure may, of course, be unpalatable. Politicians, administrators and educational experts have their opinions about reforms in society and in education, and will therefore view some manifestations of parent demands with distaste and the whole movement with suspicion. Parents are not necessarily progressive or concerned about other sections of society, and it is always possible to find pressure groups who through their resourceful campaigning have significantly worsted less articulate people. As well as groups fighting for comprehensive schools, there are others fighting to save grammar schools and their own social advantages. As well as CASE with its socialist inclinations there is the NEA with its conservative individualism. The NUT, in a pamphlet published in December 1972 called *What is Mrs Thatcher up to?*, pointed out that by upholding local objections she had saved ninety-two grammar schools and that this was 'not a policy in keeping with the need of the times and the mood of the public'.

Of all the issues perhaps the one which arouses the most venom among affected parents is that of choice of school. When a child is allocated to a school against the wishes of the parent, it will seem to be the most diabolical exercise in bureaucracy, an offence against inalienable freedoms and rights. Quite why this should be so in a system of universal state education would be obscure but for the fact that some schools are patently worse than others and that in a smaller number of cases schools are as good but different. It may also be part of a middle-class tradition of making an effort for one's child and, until comparatively recently, paying for one's child's secondary education. It has, however, been likened as a right to that of choice of religion. And perhaps parents' fear of their children falling in with the wrong set is as near to a fear of damnation as there is in this secular society.

More freedom of choice can be argued for in consumerism fashion: if parents are free to choose, then unpopular – and by this assumption bad – schools would lose pupils and their inadequacies would be made obvious and public. One headteacher, Dr Rhodes Boyson of Highbury Grove, wrote in *Education* (18 July 1969), of the value of the process to parents:

> Over the last few weeks I have been interviewing parents and their sons for entry to my school in September and I realized even more how parents' free selection of a school brings personal dignity to them and full involvement with the school. Ninety-eight per cent of parents arrived promptly for their interviews and in well over half of the interviews both parents attended, the husband taking the morning or afternoon away from work for this special occasion. On a number of occasions other adults came with the parents, especially where a cousin or a neighbour's son had already attended the school.
> Parents really are ready for full choice decisions.

Freedom of choice for parents has a very small element of protection in the Education Act 1944. Section 76 provides that children should be educated in accordance with a parent's wishes in so far as this does not conflict with the LEA's responsibilities to provide an economic service. (Freedom of choice on religious grounds is protected to a larger extent.) In practice this has been found to give little legal right, though local authorities normally try to accommodate parental choice, even though this can work against a fair allocation of pupils to all schools.

The alternatives, in addition to preventing unsatisfactory decisions by means of public protest, are either to extend freedom of choice provisions in the Education Act or to appoint a tribunal for appeals against LEA decisions. A tribunal would not only provide the benefit of appeals but would also, simply by being there, make LEAS realize that they were publicly accountable for their decisions and encourage more consideration. To make freedom of choice more effective, however, also requires more information to be given to parents in the form of leaflets about schools, visits or interviews with headmaster and teachers. Proponents of more freedom of choice found a sympathetic ear in the Conservative Secretary of

State, Mrs Thatcher, and her government intended also to establish local ombudsmen who would be able to hear certain appeals.

At a less specific level there has been a widespread recognition of the importance of good home–school relations, and both schools and parents have made contacts. Teachers and headteachers are much more likely to keep parents informed, make it easy for them to drop in for a chat, arrange meetings with form or house masters, even send out questionnaires about improvements in the school. A few schools have taken the lead in appointing teachers with special responsibility for making contacts with the homes, visiting parents and discussing problems of their children, answering questions about the school. A few others invite parents in for special lessons in the evening to keep them up-to-date with new teaching methods and subjects. In many primary schools mothers come in and help by listening to a child's reading practice, though the unions frown on the practice. The DES produced in 1968 a booklet on parent–teacher relations in primary schools.[5] Launching it, the former Labour Secretary of State, Mr Edward Short, claimed that good parent–teacher relations were the common experience in primary schools – 'unheralded, unsung and nobody knows much about it, but there it is happening all over the place'. CASE representatives at the time doubted the picture was quite so sunny; their experience was that the sum of most parent–teacher relations were fifteen-minute interviews on Open Day. CASE has through the Home and School Council published a follow-up on secondary schools[6] listing good practice and hoping thereby to encourage more.

PTAs have been encouraged. There are still many headteachers who regard them with suspicion and many, too, who regard them not as participants in the educational process but as providers of funds for swimming pools, colour TV sets or books and those teaching aids which the LEA cannot afford to supply.

The question of representation on managing and governing bodies of schools recurs throughout the discussion of parent involvement, both as a cause in itself and as a means of promoting other issues. The parent pressure groups have demanded that representatives of parents be included on these bodies as a contribution, variously, to involving parents in schools, opening the schools up to the community, ensuring that parents have a means of influencing what is done in schools and providing a formal means of protecting any rights that parents believe they have. A few local authorities have acceded to these demands in recognition of such arguments or as a machiavellian ploy, and others were encouraged to do so by the DES. Many local authorities which had one board of governors for a group of schools are reconstituting them so that each school has its own board, and then representatives of parents, teachers and, occasionally, students are appointed to the boards. Parental representation as such is limited to one or two members but the consciousness that parents are useful in theory and in practice can lead to parents being appointed to double as councillors or other representatives. A parent with particular skills such as an architect could be co-opted.

Membership of governing bodies is not enough. The governing bodies need to be given real powers and real influence over what happens in schools and not be the merely honorary ceremonial bodies which only appear on speech days and sports days. NAGM has proposed defined spending powers and responsibility for the curriculum. Parents' representatives also need to be well informed and to live up to the confidence now placed in them. (This, it should be noted, is not usually expected of the political appointees on governing bodies but parents are in the limelight.)

The demands so far considered have stopped short of involving parents in the actual educational process. They have been about supplying information, making contacts with schools and teachers and with representation, about administration and government. The experience of playgroups and the education priority areas in forging home–school links has proved that parents are not only useful contributors but also gain educationally and socially from their involvement. The report of the action-research projects in five EPSs investigated parents' attitudes to school:[7]

> Most parents are profoundly interested in their children's educational and social chances. . . . Most parents have a high regard and respect for schools, but however they admire the school they cannot always emulate it. Almost by definition, the E.P.A. parent is himself a school failure who perhaps neither enjoyed nor understood his own school. Today the whole process is even more confusing, with sophisticated and unfamiliar teaching methods, so that parents hesitate to interfere and are forced back to an implicit and uncomprehending trust. There are of course apathetic parents just as there are

lethargic teachers. Again some take school for granted, as a chore, as a sort of junior national service. . . . Whatever they think there is a general tendency for educational matters to be left to the school. The object of home–school links is to increase the educational understanding of the parent and the social understanding of the teacher.

EPA projects experimented with making links through pre-school groups, through appointing home–school liaison teachers, through encouraging parents to visit schools, through home visiting and through organizing exhibitions, 'education shops' and advice centres. Community activities inside the schools were encouraged. In Liverpool, as the project's director, Eric Midwinter, describes,[8] parents visited the classroom for coffee mornings and were sent school newsletters. The project organized exhibitions of school work in local shops and a display in a local department store. Dr Midwinter reckons that the communication established demonstrates the potential of parent–teacher partnership. He concludes:[9]

> There is no gainsaying that, for full home/school interrelation, the parent must eventually observe or, preferably, participate in the educational process. The Project has undeniably shown that the class is the most profitable focus for this exercise, with teacher and children inviting parents to join them regularly for half-day sessions. This began as 'coffee mornings', but widened encouragingly into the afternoon and evening. . . . Most schools plumped for the parents joining their children working in groups and the creation thereby of a valued social-cum-educational experience for everyone.

From the point of view of parent involvement, there are signs that playgroups are more productive than nursery schools. The EPA's report found so, though qualified this by saying they were often poorly organized. The organizer of the Huddersfield and District Pre-School Playgroups Association, Mrs Jean Brown, wrote in the *Guardian* (9 January 1973):

> I am constantly amazed and delighted at the way 'ordinary mums' want positively to be involved with their child's learning. With support and encouragement this desire is maintained (in playgroups), but the minute a child enters school the mother is politely but firmly excluded from the action.

Just as freedom of choice is a sensitive issue between parents and local authorities, so decision-making on the curriculum is a sensitive issue between parents and teachers. Teachers traditionally are accorded the right to teach what and how they decide, concepts of academic freedom and professional expertise being interwoven, as was discussed in chapter 5. Yet, arguments for community schools, imply some control or influence over the curriculum and teaching methods. However, although a place on the governing body gives nominal control over the curriculum, it is assumed in practice that it is best to leave teachers to trust their judgment and that normally the headteacher makes the crucial decisions. Any move into this area by outside bodies is regarded with suspicion and hostility by teachers. Teacher unions have found an ally in local authorities to resist any central government interference in curriculum matters, for example as they resisted the Curriculum Study Group when set up in 1962 as a 'commando-like' unit of the ministry of education. They have resisted moves from parents and public to involvement in curricular decisions.

Parents organizations have therefore to tread carefully. PTAs have foundered on the suspicion by teachers that parents are trying to interfere or to tell them what to do. The CASE demands that schools should be opened up to the community and yet it qualifies its statement on control of the curriculum:[10]

> We accept that decisions on curricula are a professional
> responsibility of teachers; however we also believe that the
> curriculum should not remain the exclusive province of teachers
> and other professional educationists. We believe that
> education is a total process, involving the home and the
> school, and that active and informed parental support for the
> work of the school is of crucial importance at every stage.

If the community school developed in the EPA projects is to be taken seriously, it depends upon community influence on the curriculum and not just the teachers' perception of what the community wants. At present one of the only ways in which a teacher's work is scrutinized is in examination passes – which ignores his non-examination classes. It is hard to see why teachers should remain unaccountable for their teaching, though their unions will defend their right to be so. Central and local government may determine the reorganization of the school system for the benefit of the community but with no sanction that the school internally operates to the same effect; a comprehensive school may be established but its internal organization and the attitudes of head and teachers may be rigorously élitist – with as damaging effects on the less successful pupils as in the former secondary modern. New ideas are introduced into the schools by a haphazard process which may or may not relate to the needs of society. CASE speaks of 'a concern that the educational system must be more responsive to an increasingly complex and fast-moving society' and sees the involvement of the community as an instrument of this.

The trust placed in teachers and the efforts to remove them from the pressures of society leave them open to other pressures – those of their own profession and careers. Obviously they are subject to the opinions of their colleagues, for ill as well as good. But often career advancement may lie in concentrating on academic teaching and on success and experience with top-stream children. Less able children are easily given second best, and society or public authorities are unable to enforce their willingness to help them.

References

1 R. Pedley, *The Comprehensive School*, Penguin, Harmondsworth, revised edn, 1969.
2 Plowden Report: *Children and their Primary Schools*, HMSO, London, 1967.
3 Ibid., pp. 30 and 35.
4 E. Midwinter, *Priority Education*, Penguin, Harmondsworth, 1972, p. 106.
5 *Education Survey No. 5: Parent–Teacher Relations in Primary Schools*, HMSO, London, 1968.
6 A. Lingard and John Allard, *Parent/Teacher Relations in Secondary Schools*, Home and School Council, 1972.
7 A. H. Halsey, *Educational Priority: EPA Problems and Policies*, vol. 1, HMSO, London, 1972, p. 118.
8 Midwinter, op. cit.
9 Ibid., p. 166.
10 *Parents and the Major New Education Act*, CASE, 1969.

11 An open system

Education has been seen as an instrument of social reform. Education has been made more available – or, more accurately, schools have been expanded – with the intention of providing a fairer education service and a better society. Arguments to this effect are based on a number of political beliefs, variously, for example, that no bright child should be hindered by social circumstances from benefiting from education, that all children should be equal initially, or that all children should have an equal chance as a result of school. These and numerous other conceptions of education may be intended to produce either egalitarian or meritocratic societies. A common denominator is the idea of equality of opportunity.

The conclusions of research into the extent to which education has provided increased equality of opportunity are not encouraging. The figures indicate that the class bias of education is largely maintained, that, for example, the proportion of children from working-class homes who go to university is no higher now than it was half-a-century ago. The popular mood – reinforced by scare stories like those about unemployed graduates during 1972 – has become disillusioned, a disillusion stepped up to frustration among that majority of the population who do not succeed in schools and for whom schools seem to offer little but unattainable examination passes. It seems less and less likely that the schools can solve society's social problems. Research indicates that social factors, such as deprivation in early childhood, have a dominating effect upon education whereas education does not manage to overcome social factors. Thus within the effort being made on behalf of education, greater attention has to be paid to social and class background of pupils and a programme of positive discrimination introduced. At the same time the fashionable focus of public concern has shifted from education to environment and planning, to ecology and pollution.

There is, however, a growing interest in education from a rather different direction, that is in education as an institution in itself rather than as an instrument of social reform. The growing interest is in the distribution of power within the education system and in the means of influencing decisions. This is prompted by various factors: the growth of consumerism, more widespread demands for democracy and participation, the assumption that education is no longer a charity, a dole, but a service which users and ratepayers should hold accountable. The topics which prompt this interest may be as idiosyncratic as an economic or philosophic objection to, for example, school uniform, to a larger dissatisfaction with the schools, to a perception of injustice or more vaguely a growth in awareness and articulacy among sections of society. Thus the education system has been exposed to increasing pressures from parents and other groups. Pressure groups have formed in the wake of disillusion with the political parties and increasing confidence in group action and, in some cases, militancy.

Some of these pressures from outside the education service have been justified by educational arguments, for example, that it is beneficial to the child to involve the parent. As such, they have to a limited extent proved acceptable to the education service. Rather more generally, however, they have seemed a challenge to the establishment. Educational administration, both in its elected representatives and officials, has traditionally been suspicious of such groups. It tends to perceive pressure groups as representing sectional and selfish interests in contrast to its own more neutral, integrated view.

The question is then posed as to how much benefit the service as a whole gains by paying attention to the demands from outside groups, the protests and the demands for representation and participation. It is true that at present most of these groups are relatively small, as compared to the electorate or the whole constituency of parents. It is true that, if one takes a fixed viewpoint, these groups have worked for good and ill: campaigns to promote comprehensive education have been countered by more virulent campaigns to save grammar schools.

It is by no means clear that increased involvement of parents will encourage progressive schemes. More than a hundred grammar schools have been saved to wreck comprehensive schemes by virtue of taking note of parental protests. The freedom of choice movement makes it difficult for a local authority to ensure that its comprehensive schools do all include a fair spread of ability, bright children as well as dull. Parents' interest in education seems to many headmasters limited to the number of examination passes their children achieve. The influential parents' pressure groups on the other hand tend to be more progressive in their policies and in the demands they make to central and local government, demanding less competition, more open access to schools and greater democracy within them. One of the bases for community schools is in the value of parental involvement in helping to form more relevant, less academic curricula. Thus greater parental participation is proposed from both the right and the left of the political spectrum, clouding the different motives and the contribution they will make to the education service.

There is every justification for regarding increased parent participation with suspicion. There can never be, however, any justification for refusing it. Parents should have, by right and for political expediency, a greater say in what happens in schools. This requires both formal representation and access to means of consultation and protest.

It has never been clear whether society becomes more democratic out of conviction or expediency: have greater numbers of the population gained the vote because it was realized that this was the basis of a just society or because the protests of the unenfranchised became inconvenient? Protest groups argue for the right of people to join in making decisions about their communities and their institutions, but in practice the institutions holding power are likely to be machiavellian and wait until the strength of the demands can no longer be ignored. It is the same with parental participation, and the demands of parents now force their way into recognition. A parallel case is that of student representation in colleges and universities. Repeated and increasingly vehement protests led to students gaining representation on some university and college bodies, and then it was often reported by those who had previously been in sole authority that the newcomers were 'really quite sensible' or 'actually rather bored by the whole process'. After a while these comments about the contribution made by the newly enfranchised become irrelevant, just as would be an argument about whether women are useful members of the electorate.

Increased parental participation should not give rise to fears that the sectional interests of particular groups of parents will take over the service. It is more likely – to be machiavellian – that formal representation reduces the demonstration and vocal protests which might otherwise force the administration's hand. The education system has too many checks and balances, too much dissipation of power for the introduction of parent representatives on to governing bodies and education committees and into other forms of consultation to throw the whole out of gear. It is always possible that at some time in the future one would argue for additional administrative and professional and less parental and public influence, but at present with the service dominated by administrative measures and by a professional establishment it would be difficult to overdo parental representation.

Students and teachers are also increasingly vocal in demands for representation. It is part of the same social movement as that for parental participation but it by no means leads to the same thing. Teachers' interests as professionals are often hostile to parents. The problem is to recognize their distinct interests along with those of parents and to establish institutions to reconcile them.

But, aside from discussion of rights and practical politics, the test of the existing system must be its achievements. The question which has to be asked is whether the operation of the education service by the existing forces of central and local government and teachers has produced what society has wanted. The question is far too sweeping to give a straightforward or entirely truthful answer, but in any case it would have to be a negative answer. The statistics of the education service show a huge expansion but they do not show a huge success. One cannot deny the advances, the higher standards, the extra schooling, the proportion of the age-group going to university, the increase in equipment and buildings provided. One cannot deny the seriousness and effort put in against all the odds by civilized and humane administrators and teachers. But nor can one find evidence that the school system has expanded equality of opportunity; in other words it has failed in what appears to be its principal social objective.

Why have the good intentions of the education service and educationalists not been realized? There are two equally unpalatable reasons: because the education service is unable to achieve them; or because it was not seriously intended to achieve them – because in other words we were duped. The education service seems unable to implement its own policies. Nearly ten years after comprehensive schools were accepted by the consensus of political parties and those engaged in education there are still less than half the country's secondary age children going to them. Before that, secondary modern schools had not been given facilities and esteem equal to those of the grammar schools. In post-school education, the polytechnics, intended to be the peak of the more democratic further education service, have become more like universities, losing their working-class students, dropping part-time and vocational studies, becoming less open institutions. It seems unlikely that those children who have to stay at school for the extra year will generally get the facilities and opportunities to learn which are appropriate for them. There are many other examples of failures within the education service, and the annoyance of writers, researchers and theorists is not new, no more than is the depression of teachers and administrators or the potentially more violent frustration of those who suffer from them.

The education service also tends to discourage aspects of learning which do not fit its conventional institutions. Despite nominal support for further education, when there is a shortage of resources it is further education, the non-statutory service, which is cut back. Despite evidence of the value of parental involvement in playgroups, plans for pre-school education in the White Paper will encourage nursery classes and nursery schools. Demands to extend opportunity in education are usually couched in terms of expansion of existing institutions.

There are two factors to consider, one is the way in which the system works, the other the ways in which factors external to education impinge upon it. What do these suggest for the effectiveness of the education service?

The education system operates through a complicated distribution of powers. It endeavours through consultation and negotiation to operate by a consensus and to maintain a partnership of central and local government. Central and local government prefer to operate through seemingly uncontroversial administrative measures rather than through public statements of objectives. It is administrative in two ways: it leaves the central issues of curriculum and teaching to schools and teachers, hoping only to set the framework in which they can give of their best; it prefers to use administrative measures or informal contacts rather than statements of public policy with their attendant commitment and controversy. One effect is that it becomes difficult to oppose or to argue on issues, either because what is happening becomes only slowly evident or because the assumptions or political bases for the decisions are not stated. Another effect is that because the objectives and the policy are not stated, it is difficult to assess whether what it was – covertly – hoped to achieve has been achieved. This seems to have a conservative effect by allowing any proposals to backslide into conventional ways rather than having to stand by their intentions. There is, too, the danger that self-restraint is often more cautious than public constraints, and this again tends to the conservative.

There are special effects for those people and organizations outside the main body of opinion. First, it makes it more difficult to find out what is happening and to contribute ideas or opposition. It is difficult to know at what stage one can contribute, in the sense both of when it is formally proper and when tactically useful to do so. Thus protest tends to arise after all the effective decisions have been made in the administrative machinery and therefore tends to be ineffective. Second, it makes it difficult to contribute radical ideas, ideas which do not fit in with the given framework of the decisions and the system. It is even more difficult to contribute radical ideas because the system is predominantly paternalist. The inertia of the education service is caused in part by its inability to discuss radical ideas within the framework of its operation.

The second main factor is that of external circumstances. The disillusion with education has been joined by more determined arguments from the EPA experience that education cannot hope to cure all social ills. In this they have a link with those conservative forces who, having a narrow – academic – view of education, never thought it could cure anything in the first place. The education service itself has moved towards positive discrimination and by the EPAs and urban programme to involvement with social problems but effective links with other social services are limited.

Education only deals with its successes. It does more and more for those whom it has favoured; the child who is academically bright tends to get better teachers, is better thought of and does better still; he stays on at school, goes to college and university, all of which cost progressively more. Education's failures sink out of sight – and then later become problems for social services, courts and psychiatric hospitals. But not only does education ignore them, it also ignores ideas from external non-academic sources which might improve the situation. Some of the most interesting developments relevant to education are outside the scope of education authorities, in the Department of Employment's retraining and industrial training, in community work, in the Social Services Departments' handling of problem children and families. These are all outside the experience of the education service, although free schools may tap some of these interests.

Yet the education service is proud of the battle it won to keep education committees a statutory requirement under the new Local Government Act distinct from other local government services. It fought in defence of a principle of education being a special service for every child, when manifestly education is something which benefits the few. It did this to protect itself from outside interference. The direction indicated by community schools, by knowledge of the importance of social factors is, however, different. If the schools should open themselves to the community, the education service, too, has to be joined to other community services. One of the lessons which one would hope is learnt is that there are other ways of learning than in schools, the administration of which is the basis of the education service. Different concepts of learning and education have been developed which point to the value of more open institutions and to working with other agencies in social reform. The education service should not continue to isolate itself. The learning society in order to establish democratic education would integrate learning institutions into society and would make the participation of students in decision-making essential.

What emerges from all these considerations? The following reforms in the areas of public participation are proposed for criticism. They are interrelated but not necessarily interdependent.

The problem of reconciling the different interests of parents, teachers, students and public is best met by establishing governing bodies to include representatives of all these constituencies. They should be half representative of the school – students, teachers and parents – and half of the local authority and outside interests. They should have real and defined powers which would enable them to exercise some management functions and to be an effective political body. Governing bodies as well as providing an instrument of participation and accountability could usefully contribute to making the education service more public and its decision-making more accessible. In making policies for schools they should engage in public discussions and publish (or have published) reports on the implementation of policies.

Dissatisfaction with administration should be met through setting up tribunals or local ombudsmen so that there are procedures for appeal against decisions of the local authority and governing body. This also would contribute to the recognition by local authorities and schools of their accountability to the public and to the opening up of administrative processes.

The schools should be opened up to the community and play a part in social reform by providing community-based learning. The reformed governing bodies should take decision-making powers on the curriculum and encourage innovations through public discussion. Reliance on professional teachers should be reduced by providing more opportunity for other people to teach or to assist learning in schools. Reliance on schools should be reduced by increasing support for further and adult education. The education service should co-ordinate with social services.

The administration of education should be made more public, and some of the measures above would contribute to this. Administrative measures must operate in such a way that they are available for public inspection. There should be no confidentiality, except as a last resort in personal matters. Whatever can be done to change paternalist attitudes and the instinctive withholding of information must be done.

The education service must not rely on administrative measures to introduce its notional reforms, as doing so has resulted in the exclusion of the public and in the non-implementation of the reforms. It should express its policies in terms both of objectives (social or educational) and of administrative measures so that they may be argued over and tested for success or failure. Public statements should be encouraged and private bargaining discouraged; the education service should shed some of its complexities and subtleties.

Education is a public service and should act like one. A democratic education service should do what the people want and do what is best for them – perhaps the way in which different people interpret that as a conflict is the test of their politics.

Further reading

Education Committees Yearbook, Councils and Education Press, London.
An annual publication with addresses of all LEA's universities and colleges, unions and pressure groups. This is where to find the latest addresses of the pressure and interest groups described in chapter 4.
(A reminder when writing for information to voluntary bodies – always enclose a stamped addressed envelope for the reply.)

J. Stone and F. Taylor, *Handbook for Parents with a Handicapped Child*, Home and School Council, 1972.
A directory of services and organizations for handicapped children. From CASE publications, 17 Jacksons Lane, Billericay, Essex, or NCPTA, 1 White Avenue, Northfleet, Gravesend, Kent.

T. Burgess, *A Guide to English Schools*, Penguin, Harmondsworth, revised edn., 1973.
A handbook to what the law says and how the education system is administered with explanations of different types of schools.

J. Pratt, T. Burgess, R. Allemano and M. Locke, *Your Local Education*, Penguin, Harmondsworth, 1973.
A guide to the different levels of provision by LEAs with sections on local authority finance and on the implications for a child's education.

G. Taylor and J. B. Saunders, *The New Law of Education*, Butterworth, London, 1971 (7th edn).
Educational legislation from the Education Act 1944 until recently is reproduced together with a commentary.

Further reading

J. S. Maclure, *Educational Documents – England and Wales 1816–1968*, Methuen, London, 1969 (2nd edn).
Extracts from the major reports and legislation for the past 150 years.

Addresses

Confederation for the Advancement of State Education
Secretary: Mrs Barbara Bullivant, 81 Rustlings Road, Sheffield
S11 7AB

National Education Association
General Secretary: Mrs Ruth Bradbury, Highcroft, Tewin Close,
Tewin Wood, Hertfordshire

National Confederation of Parent–Teacher Associations
General Secretary: John Hale, 1 White Avenue, Northfleet, Gravesend, Kent

Advisory Centre for Education
32 Trumpington Street, Cambridge

Home and School Council
Secretary: Mrs Barbara Bullivant, 81 Rustlings Road, Sheffield
S11 7AB

National Association of Governors and Managers
Secretary: Mrs Anne Sofer, 46 Regent's Park Road, London
NW1 7SX

Campaign for Comprehensive Education
Secretary: 123 Portland Road, London W11

STOPP
Secretary: Miss Gene Adams, 12 Lawn Road, London NW3

Addresses

National Campaign for Nursery Education
Chairman: Mrs E. M. Osborn, Anlaby Lodge, Teddington, Middlesex

Nursery Schools Association
89 Stamford Street, London SE1 9ND

Pre-School Playgroups Association
Alford House, Aveline Street, London SE11 5DJ

Note
Latest addresses can be checked in current issues of the *Education Committees Year Book* (Councils and Education Press).

Index

Index

Index

Index

Index

UNIVERSITY LIBRARY NOTTINGHAM